WINNING CONCEPTS
FOR COACHING
WINNING FOOTBALL

LEARN FROM THE MASTERS

Milt Theodosatos

authorHOUSE®

AuthorHouse™
1663 Liberty Drive, Suite 200
Bloomington, IN 47403
www.authorhouse.com
Phone: 1-800-839-8640

First published by AuthorHouse   1/6/2009

ISBN: 978-1-4389-2108-2 (sc)

Printed in the United States of America
Bloomington, Indiana

This book is printed on acid-free paper.

DEDICATION

- -

This book is dedicated to my wife of 51 years,
Georgia Elizabeth Baker Theodosatos.
"She has allowed me to be me."

WHY ANOTHER BOOK ON FOOTBALL AND HOW THIS BOOK CAN HELP YOU!

If you are a coach or a fan, I hope to present information that is _different_ from the ordinary. Information that I have learned over a 47 year coaching career by being a Student of the Game.

This book is NOT about X's and O's. This book will discuss concepts. This book will question some of the philosophy that is used today as compared to the lessons taught by the Legends of the Game of yesterday. This book will try to explain …….*Why games are won and Why games are lost.* In answering this thought, I will express my opinion based on the teachings and experience I have had in the past 47 years.

Hopefully this book with give you the reader a FRESH in-sight into the game that you may NOT be aware of.….. OR…...it may reinforce information you already are aware of and use.

Hopefully, this book will be informative and FUN to read.

ABOUT THE AUTHOR
COACH MILT THEODOSATOS

Theodosatos was born and raised in New York City. Going into his junior year in high school, he and his parents moved to Long Island and "Theo" attended Mineola High School where he lettered in both football and baseball.

After a career in both football and baseball at Springfield College in Springfield, Massachusetts, "Theo" started his 47year *Journey in the Football World.*

Forty-Two of those years, "Theo" served as head coach. Thirty-nine years as a head coach on the secondary school level and one year as Head Coach of the Luebeck Cougars in the German Football League in Germany. His final two years at the helm were with the Tennessee Valley Vipers (Huntsville, Alabama) in the arena2 Professional Indoor Football League

"Theo" has been labeled the "rebuilder" for taking over losing programs and turning them into contenders, winners and Champions.

Seventeen coaching stops along the way. He has a head coaching record of 205-176-6 with coaching stints in New York, New Jersey, Oklahoma,

Alabama, Texas, New Hampshire and Luebeck, Germany.

"Theo" had head coaching stints in New Jersey at Plainfield (twice), Bishop Ahr, Sayreville, Rahway, Johnson Regional, Madison, and Monroe.

Theodosatos, in the twi- light of his career, then moved on to the professional level in the arena2 league. He has served as assistant head coach for the Tennessee Valley Vipers in 2003 and 2004 as well as the Rio Grande Valley Dorados in 2005. He had the highest win percentage of any arena 2 professional football league assistant head coach (Won 39 Lost 15) with three playoff appearances and two Conference Championships)

In 2006 he was called on to be head coach of the Tennessee Valley Vipers, his old team in Huntsville, Alabama. Only problem, the job called for "Theo" to pick up the pieces at the end of the 2006 season(last 6 games) when the present coach was fired. He also served as head coach in 2007.

He is the only high school coach in the State of New Jersey that has brought 5 different programs to the State Playoffs. Plainfield in 1976, and 1978, Bishop Ahr in 1983, Johnson Regional in 1991, Plainfield again (2nd tour) in 1996 and Madison in 1998 (State Champions).

His 1976 Plainfield High School team was the first high school team to play in Giants Stadium and WIN in the Play-offs!

"Theo" coached the victorious New Jersey All Star squad in the 2000 Governors Bowl against New York State.

Theodosatos has also coached baseball, basketball and track and earned nine Coach of the Year honors in all sports (5 in football).

One of the great honors that "Theo" has received was his selection into the New Jersey Football Coaches Hall of Fame.

"Theo" was instrumental in helping the New Jersey Coaches Association to achieve the expansion of the 10 game season schedule and the development of the play-off system.

"Theo" is especially proud of all the players he has sent on to play college football as well as the 40 plus players who have gone onto different levels of professional football.

Theodosatos has spoken at dozens of clinics throughout the eastern seaboard. His favorite topic is "Motivation" and "Developing Positive Mind Set".

Theodosatos and Georgia, his wife of 50 years, reside in Huntsville, Alabama.

ACKNOWLEDGEMENTS

-- --

It is important that I try to acknowledge as many of the people that I can remember, who through the years have influenced my learning of the great game of football.

Starting with my high school coaches, Ken "Dutch" Hafner and Bruce Gehrke. My college coaches Ozzie Solem and Ted "Tiger" Dunn. And.....the unbelievable list of high school, college and professional football coaches.

Through the years I have attended football clinics, college spring practices, professional pre-season camps, and have learned from some of the greatest coaches the game has ever produced.

In this book, when I can, I will give credit to the coach from whom I first learned a specific concept. I will try my best to give credit to where credit belongs. The list of coaches reads like a Hall of Fame list;

George Allen, Bear Bryant, Vince Lombardi, Bobby Dodd, Jake Gaither,Buddy Parker, Don Coryell, Jack Curtice, Ara Parseghian, Paul Brown, Chuck Mather, Tony Mason, LaVell Edwards, John McKay, Eddie Erdalatz, Bud Wilkenson, Gomer Jones, Lee Corso, Darry Royal, Woody Hayes, Red Blake, Homer Smith, Bob Blackman, Leo Strange, Lou

Thom Howard, Lou Amonson, Forrest Evasheski, Murray Warmarth, Johnny Majors, Bill Parcells, Bill Walsh, Ozzie Solem, Ted "Tiger" Dunn ....the list can go on and on.

Please understand that after 47 years of coaching, it is very difficult to pin point exactly where I learned some of the information presented in this book.

I would also like to give special thanks to high school coaches whom I have had the pleasure of coaching with and who have helped with this book by giving their evaluation; Clint Jones, Plainfield, N.J., Jim Griffin, Monroe Township, N.J., Kurt Page, St. Thomas H.S., Houston, Texas, and Tony Aschettino, Bishop Ahr H.S., North Edison, N.J.

CONTENTS

MORE GAMES ARE LOST THAN WON!

I learned this concept back in the early 1960's from the coaching legend Paul "Bear" Bryant during one of his clinic talks. He stressed that mistakes,…penalties…*BREAKDOWNS*…. was the biggest reason why teams lost. Thus, the "Bear" said, " More Games are Lost Than Won!".

Either offensive, defensive or kicking game *BREAKDOWNS* resulted in a team losing.

It wasn't because one team had better talent than the other. Because…many times, teams with lesser talent end up winning the game.

Why?

The Bear stressed BREAKDOWNS.

This book will address mostly OFFENSIVE BREAK-DOWNS. After forty-seven years of coaching, it is this coach's opinion that it is on the offensive side of the ball where most games are lost.

PLAYER BREAKDOWNS

Teams create their own *Breakdowns.* Players create their own *Breakdowns.*

Breakdowns in the form of penalties...off-sides....holding... fumbles.........missed assignments...bad decisions... etc.,etc..

COACH BREAKDOWNS

Coaches call bad plays for the situation at hand. Coaches call poor percentage plays on offense which make it *more* difficult for the offense to convert a first down or score a TD.

Coaches call poor percentage defenses which helps the offense,thus the Coach made a coaching mistake.....a *Breakdown* by the Coach. In many cases the players will get blamed for not executing, when in reality, the coach put the players in a BAD situation. A *Breakdown* by the Coach.

Remember.....a coach's MAIN responsibility is to put his players in the best position to be successful.

Teams lose rather than get beat....by MISTAKES...... BREAKDOWNS. On the field and on the SIDELINE.

SELL... DON'T TELL!

In teaching, we learned the concept....SELL..DON'T TELL! So often teachers...coaches....dictate to their teams. They lecture. They give information to their players assuming the players will learn. Though, this can be true to a certain degree, it is better if we SELL a player on an idea.

When we dictate information, we do not know if the player truly understands our point and if the player BUYS into what we are trying to teach.

We can SELL our point if we give reasons and examples and explain *Why* to support our teaching. We can SELL rather than TELL by asking questions to our players. In this way, they give feedback in regards to the information we lectured to them.

PLAYERS MUST BE TESTED TO DETERMINE IF THEY KNOW WHAT TO DO MENTALLY.

An example;

We introduce blocking assignments for a specific running play. In doing so, we do not JUST give the assignment, we tell our players WHY we are blocking the play in this manner. Then to get feedback, we ask the question to the player, "What is your assignment and why are we blocking the play this way?"

I believe that when we have INTERACTION........... COMMUNICATION between player and coach ....this is better than lecturing only.

Using this technique we get feedback from the player. The answer to the questions come from his mouth NOT mine.

I consider this to be SELLING NOT TELLING!

Learning assignments is different than memorizing assignments. In learning we have less chance of forgetting. In learning, the information is tied together with reason and logic. In memorization, it is much easier to forget.

SELL ……….DON'T TELL

LESS CHANCE FOR A MENTAL ERROR DURING A GAME.

LESS CHANCE FOR A BREAKDOWN.

There is a BIG difference-

At the end of every game, in our team meeting….I would ask our team……....whether we won or lost (it did not make any difference)….I would ask our team…

DID WE WIN OR DID THE OTHER TEAM LOSE?
DID WE BEAT THEM OR DID THEY LOSE?

There is a BIG difference.

More often than not…the response from my team would be that *they lost* through BREAKDOWNS…….and my players would count off the critical errors they made to lose the game. This is very important in my coaching.Teaching that BREAKDOWNS were the reason for the other

Team losing helped to sell my players on the need for GREAT PRACTICE... THE IMPORTANCE OF QUALITY REPS... THE IMPORTANCE OF QUALITY PRACTICE... THE IMPORTANCE OF POSITIVE REPS (NOT NEGATIVE REPS)... THE NEED TO WORK TO ELIMINATE MISTAKES... THE REASON WHY WE ALWAYS SAY AND COACH; PAY ATTENTION TO DETAIL!

Or if we lost the game, I would say;
Did *we lose* or did *we get beat*?

There is a difference............and again...more often than not our players would say....we lost..... we did not get beat. They would rattle off the things that we did to screw up. They knew that *we had control* over these errors. WE LOST!

More games are lost than won....this is what Bear Bryant was trying to emphasize and SELL!

In teaching this concept, we use this story as an example; If we played the New York Giants...we would not lose......we would get BEAT. They would kill us. They would destroy us. We do not have to worry about breakdowns because they are the Pros....they are the NFL...and we are a high school team....they would BEAT US...WE WOULD NOT LOSE...PERIOD. WE WOULD GET BEAT!

If we played the School of the Blind....

NOW UNDERSTAND THIS; They are the School of the Blind. They can not see. Thus there is no way we lose. BUT.....if we played them....and they scored more points than we did ......(impossible...they can not see)......did we lose or did we get beat?

Obviously…we LOST the game. Remember…they can not see…they are blind.

BREAKDOWNS would have lost the game for us.

I am aware that these are exaggerated examples but I use them to sell the point.

Normally we play teams that we have a chance to beat or they have a chance to beat us. They may have a better Quarterback….but we have a better Fullback. They have better linebackers…but we have a better defensive secondary. The game can go either way…for us or against us.

In the end….one team won or lost…..usually due to BREAKDOWNS.

Sometimes BREAKDOWNS are *forced by our opponent..* These types of BREAKDOWNS are different. These are forced BREAKDOWNS….. *The team losing GOT BEAT!*

Thus…..there are two types of BREAKDOWNS…..

1. The type we had control over…the type we committed by our error.

2. The type of BREAKDOWNS that our opponents forced us to commit.

These types of examples helps us sell the concept….
MORE GAMES ARE LOST THAN WON!

Knowing this concept, helps to sell our team on the need for quality practice. It makes our coaching job easier and more efficient. This concept helps to improve on the productivity of our coaching efforts. This is the reason why this concept is mentioned first. It is here where we sell the need for REPS.

We give the example; Michael Jordan…the great basketball player….did he take 10 free throws at practice or did he take 100? Does a concert pianist practice 10 minutes a day or does he practice 10 hours a day? The need for quality REPS is easy to sell when they understand this concept…

More games are lost than won!

CONTROL OR NO CONTROL

It is here where we teach our players….there are two types of experiences that we will have in sports.

- One type of experience is one in which <u>we have control over.</u>

- The second type of experience is one in which <u>we have NO control over.</u>

Our offensive BREAKDOWNS that we do on our own……. WE HAVE CONTROL OVER….

We have NO control over what the other team tries to do….no control over their size….their speed…..their attitude……no control over the officials….no control over the weather……. no control…….

Thus, let's worry ONLY about the things we do have control over. A GREAT COACHING CONCEPT!

THE 10 POSSESSION RULE

Evaluation of every possession will tell us if…..."we won or they lost…..we lost or they beat us." This evaluation will tell us where the Player Breakdowns occurred and where the Coach Breakdowns occurred.

During a game there are usually between 10 to 15 possessions. In a high school game there are usually 10 possessions. …5 in each half. In a college game or in the NFL…there may be as many as 16 possessions in one game.

The Coach needs to evaluate what happened on each and every possession both offensively and defensively and in the kicking game.

Coaches in charge of Quality Control will evaluate each possession….each play (first and ten…..2nd and short etc.) to determine why a play was successful or a failure.

- Why did we move the ball? Or… why did we get stopped?

- Did we BREAKDOWN and stop ourselves, or did our opponent stop us.

There is a big difference between both possibilities. We always have to evaluate…and ask the question. WHY?

Understanding WHY tells us WHY we succeeded for failed and WHY will help us in future planning. Understanding WHY can help us to WIN.

If we as coaches do not do this important *evaluation* then we are missing a great opportunity in learning *How to win.* Remember Chapter #1………

"More games are Lost Than Won!" We have some degree of *control* over our possessions.

3 CATEGORIES OF PLAYS

Years ago, I learned from Bobby Dodd the legendary coach from Georgia Tech, that under evaluation, we have to understand that plays are divided into 3 categories; DIRECT…… DELAYED….and SPECIAL.

Direct plays are quick hitters….the sneak….the dive….a quick trap….a toss. In the passing game….a 3 step drop ….or a quick sprintout …...a play where there is really no faking…. no delay……these are examples of *Direct plays.*

Delayed plays are usually misdirection plays. A delayed play usually fakes one way and goes the other way…...a counter…a long trap…….a bootleg….a reverse are some examples of possible delayed plays.

Special Plays are the unusual. A flea flicker…..hook and ladder…..a double reverse……a special formation……etc.

When evaluating our possessions we have to take the categories of plays into consideration. DID WE USE THE BEST POSSIBLE PLAY FOR THE SITUATION?

SOME OBSERVATIONS WHEN TEAMS STOP THEMSELVES.

Offense-

THE RUN GAME

The Run Game…..Direct or Delayed or Special- When a run play is called for, the coach has a choice. Does he call a DIRECT…DELAYED or SPECIAL play.

Down and distance will help to determine his decision. But…let's use an example. Let's start off with the offense having the ball, first and ten in the 4 down zone. Let's say….. on your opponents 20 yard line.

- Woody Hayes stressed that you should …….GO DIRECT YOUNG MAN!…..GO DIRECT. Challenge them. Shove it down their throats. Don't try to be cute with something tricky and delayed. See if they can stop you.

- Vince Lombardi said attack their best defenders. If you succeed, you beat their best and demoralize them. He said attack the strongest link in their defensive chain and destroy that link and your opponent is beat.

- Or you can attack the weakest LINK IN THE CHAIN.

Whatever decision you make, still GO DIRECT first. If your opponent is superior to you and stops any type of DIRECT play, you need to be able to use a DELAYED play....misdirection. Force the defense to fly to the first fake and counter back the other way. Take advantage of their quickness to fly to where they think the running play is going.

The errors that I have seen in the past is that some coaches try to be tricky *first* by using a DELAYED play or a SPECIAL play on first down.

So often these plays end up losing yardage and then the offensive team is in a BAD 2nd down and distance situation.

Some coaches say......"but...the defense knows or expects the play"...SO WHAT...ole Woody Hayes would say....... THEY STILL HAVE TO STOP YOU.

DID WE PASS WHEN WE SHOULD HAVE RUN?

On first down, here are the choices;

- Run the ball....DIRECT, DELAYED or SPECIAL

- Pass the football.....play action

- Pass the football….dropback...sprintout….any pass with no run fake.

Ask yourself….which is best?

- Run DIRECT…if they stop you it will most likely be for ZERO YARDS creating a 2nd and 10.

- Run DELAYED or SPECIAL…if they stop you it will most likely be for a LOSS creating a 2nd and long.

- Pass with play action. Here you are attacking the defenders that have two responsibilities….run and pass.…..the outside linebackers…corners and inside linebackers.

  They can not play the run and the pass at the same time.

  If they stop you or you stop yourself, it becomes an incomplete pass or a possible Sack for a loss.

- Pass using a dropback or sprintout…some type of a *No* fake pass play. Here, we help the defense by showing pass immediately. If we fail here it is an incomplete pass or an interception or a sack for a loss.

  Using this type of play really helps the Defense. We show pass "right now" and it makes it easier for the pass to be defended.

If we succeed with either a run or pass everyone is happy. It *appears* that the play called was a good decision because the play worked. I ask you……using percentages……which do you think is the better decision to make?

Everyone loves to throw the football. I love to throw the football. The fans love to see long passes. It is exciting. But three things cn happen when you pass and two of them are bad!

I am sure you have heard that before. BUT....***The defense must first prove that they can stop the run.***

THE QB SNEAK

The QB Sneak is the #1 play in any offensive package. The sneak possibility forces the defense to maintain defense of the A gaps. The Sneak can be a called play or a Silent Sneak.

John McCay, the great USC coach loved the Sneak. He wanted his whole team to feel that the QB was the toughest SOB they have on the team. I learned from him that you can teach your QB to use the Sneak anytime IT IS A PROPER DOWN AND DISTANCE SITUATION ......considering...time...score..etc.

The point here is to force the defense to defend the A gaps. With proper use of formation, the defense can be forced to defend 9 or 10 gaps. When you add the areas of pass defense responsibility, there are not enough defenders to defend all areas and gaps.

Back in the 1960's while coaching at Sewanhaka High School on Long Island, my QB ran 70 yards for a TD on a SNEAK.

We used a formation, spreading the defense wide. Our opponent left the middle open. Our QB called a SILENT SNEAK and the rest is history.

While coaching in Germany in the GFL, my QB ran a SNEAK from our own one yard line for nine yards and a first down. My QB almost ran for a 99 yard TD. Our offensive formation spread the defense wide and left the middle open. Only a shoestring tackle by a defensive back stopped the play from going all the way.

THE PASSING GAME

Early in the game find out if they can play pass defense! Don't wait until the end of the game to find out!

Al Davis, Oakland Raiders......always had Ken Stabler test the defense on the very first possession by throwing deep. TEST THEM. This concept is very valuable. It should be in your game plan.

Soooooooooo even though I just tried to sell you on the run game.....going direct first.....I am also trying to sell you on....*when and how to pass...* and WHY? You have to be able to pass the football successfully. If your QB doesn't have the ability to throw deep, then he better have the ability to throw short successfully.

YOU MUST BE ABLE TO PASS THE BALL SUCCESSFULLY IN THE SHORT PASSING GAME.

Years ago I took a new head coaching assignment and I hired one of the old staff's coaches as an assistant. He tried to tell me that we did not have anyone who could catch the football. WOW! What a whole bunch of crap!

As coaches we are teachers. Anyone can learn to CATCH BETTER through the use of ball drills. There are dozens of ball drills that can be done during the season and in the off season to get your players to CATCH THE BALL BETTER.

NO EXCUSES. YOU HAVE TO BE ABLE TO THROW THE BALL

SUCCESSFULLY IN THE SHORT PASSING GAME.

DO YOU GAMBLE OR INVEST?

- Gamblers lose most of the time. Gamblers like long odds. Gamblers like the lottery. "Yea"- "Maybe I will win a million dollars."

- Investors are the WINNERS more often than not. Investors like to invest in people like Bill Gates!!! Invest in percentages.

Some years ago I read a thesis, a survey of possibilities of percentages in offensive football. The study showed two important points that I will always remember;

a. After studying hundreds of games, the study showed that if the offensive team gets the ball, first and ten inside their own 10 yard line, the chances of them marching down to score a TD is 90-1, unless a long gainer of 30 yards or more is made by the offense. The offense ......WILL ALMOST ALWAYS BREAKDOWN on it's own. (Fumble, penalties, interception, missed assignment, etc,)

b. The study also showed that an offensive drive, a possession, of more than 12 plays will STOP itself with BREAKDOWNS.......unless the offense has a long gainer of 30 yards or more.

Through the years I have had great fun keeping track of these two facts while I watch a football game either in person or on TV. Time and again, the information holds up. This information is important while evaluating possessions.

CONVERSION ROUTES

Conversion routes are a MUST. Years ago, players were taught pass patterns. These pass patterns were what I call..... IN CEMENT. The receiver had to run a certain number of yards....make a cut and go to a specific location. I learned from Coach Jack Curtice, his philosophy of the passing Game. He was one of the coaches who introduced CONVERSION routes. His influence changed the way pass patterns are executed today.

Today, there are still times when it is necessary to have a pattern in cement....such as an out pattern. But, receivers need to learn how to *Read on the Run.* Receivers need to read if the defense is a zone or man cover or combo. Receivers need to be able to ADJUST their pattern to get OPEN.

CONVERSION patterns are a MUST in your passing game package.

BACKSIDE......BACKSIDE......BACKSIDE!

We use a pattern for our backside receiver, whether it be the tight end or a split end or flanker. We call this pattern our SAFETY pattern. The receiver is taught to run through the middle 1/3rd of the defensive secondary. He will *Read on the Run.* He can convert this pattern to a skinny post, a deep crossing pattern, a shallow crossing pattern, an under pattern, or he can cross into a open spot in the defensive secondary. It is his choice. As the backside receiver he is almost always open regardless what the coverage is.

Let me use this example.

One of our formations will have two immediate receivers to either the right or left and only one receiver to the opposite side. You may call this a right or left formation or strong side- weak side.

Towards the two receiver side, we are using a 2 man pattern. The outside receiver is doing a curl pattern. The inside receiver is doing a wheel pattern.

These two front side receivers may be covered but I am telling you, almost always, our backside receiver is open. We teach our QB to read the onside, but if he is not 100% sure, quickly go to the BACKSIDE.….BACKSIDE…

BACKSIDE.

In practice,when we REP pass patterns,I will get behind the QB and *shout out load,* as a reminder..........BACKSIDE…. BACKSIDE….BACKSIDE!

We want our QBs to get programmed to think BACKSIDE. We teach our QBs to make a ONSIDE read that has to be 100% true in their judgment. 99% is not good enough. If they make a *quick read and if they are not 100% sure of a throw to the onside, go BACKSIDE immediately.*

Our QB's are taught to THROW THE BALL AWAY if they are not 100% sure of a pass to the BACKSIDE. (unless they can pull the ball down and run for positive yardage)

Almost all of our patterns have the ability to be a CONVERSION route.

HOT RECEIVER SYSTEM-

In teaching the passing game, a *Hot Receiver System* must be in place.

We teach our receivers when they line up on the line of scrimmage, they are to read the defense from the inside-out. Once our receivers leave the line of scrimmage on the snap, they are to read inside linebackers (we do not count the Middle LB in the 43 …he is counted for in our blocking scheme for the front 5 offensive linemen and should be taken care of if he is on a blitz.)

If an inside linebacker(such as a 44 defense) on the side of the receiver blitzes, that receiver is to convert his pattern over the open area the linebacker vacated. We use a call to communicate to the entire team that a

Hot Receiver situation exists. Our lineman immediately cut block their defenders to get hands down.

An example of a *Hot* call to our left could be ICE. A call to our right could be THUNDER. This call is made by one of three or by all three of the following players;

The receiver converting his pattern. The lineman who sees the LB Blitz. Or, a running back who sees the Blitz.

It is important for the QB to pre-snap read the defense and ANTICIPATE a possible Blitz from anywhere.

We teach our QBs to know all blocking assignments. In this way, the QB can pre-snap read the defense and ANTICIPATE where the blitz will come from and if our blocking scheme will hold up and account for every defender rushing the QB.

On every pass play, we teach ANTICIPATION of a blitz and the possible use of our *Hot Receiver System.*

EVERY PASS.....IS A POSSIBLE HOT RECEIVER CALL!

AREA OF THE MOST MISTAKES

Watching football over the years, I have learned that it is the lack of a well executed Hot Receiver System that demonstrates the area where the most mistakes occur in the passing game. Either the receiver screws up by not reading the blitz or the QB doesn't read and ANTICIPATE. Or.....there is no Hot Receiver System in place. I have seen this happen over and over again....every Saturday and Sunday.

Sometimes, the TV analyst will make a comment that the receiver didn't pick up the HOT read.

It is important, at this time, to mention a very important coaching point when it comes to evaluation of personnel. The lack of paying attention to detail is a mental skill that is over looked too often in evaluating a player. Too often, we as coaches select a player based on physical skills primarily.

How do you evaluate COMMON SENSE?

How do you evaluate ANTICIPATION?

The answer to these two questions is obvious. *Only by seeing the athlete perform!*

THE HISTORY OF FOOTBALL IS LOADED WITH PLAYERS WHO WERE A STEP SLOWER...A BIT SMALLER...BUT THEY MADE PLAYS. THEY HAD GREAT COMMON SENSE (Savvy) AND GREAT ANTICIPATION.

In the passing game, poorly executed Hot Receivers is a major reason for Offensive Possessions to BREAKDOWN. When the defense rushes 6 and the offense only has 5 blockers, there is one man that is not being blocked. Remember, *"More Games are Lost Than Won!"*

QUARTERBACK ESCAPE LANES-

Back in the late 1960's I started to use a defensive scheme where I would assign one defender to be responsible for the possibility of the QB pulling the ball down and running when he received great pass rush pressure and was forced to ESCAPE from the pressure.

I called this scheme...*Pick Up.* One defensive lineman was taught to attack his offensive blocker and make sure the offensive blocker stayed with him.

(This was important because we did not want the offensive lineman to slip off our defensive lineman and try to pick up a blitzing linebacker....this would destroy our attempt at rushing 6 vs. 5 or 7 vs. 6).

The defensive lineman would hold his ground and read the backfield for the possibility of a running back releasing for a Pass (possible screen)....or the QB running one of the ESCAPE LANES.

This scheme enabled us to stunt one extra man than the offense had blockers. This pressure forced QB's to scramble and try to ESCAPE.

Conversely.....we taught our QB where the ESCAPE LANES were and to use them if and when necessary.

As the years went by and more teams started using this *Pick Up* technique, the word *SPY* was introduced. We teach our offense and defense the location of possible QB ESCAPE LANES.

Today, it appears that many teams STILL do not use this SPY technique to stop the QB from a run possibility when he decides to pull the ball down and not pass. I say this because while watching college games and the NFL on TV, many QB's score TD's down in the Red Zone by pulling the ball down and hitting the ESCAPE lanes only to have NO ONE assigned to pick them up.

RESULT.....TD for the QB.

ESCAPE LANES exist vs. every defensive front. We teach our QBs where the possible LANES may be.

Michael Vick, of the Atlanta Falcons, has made a career of running the ball through these LANES.

We love playing against defensive teams that are not prepared to pick up our QB with a *SPY.*

In the sprint-out passing game, we teach our QB that there is a great ESCAPE LANE to the backside. Thus, once the QB sprints out and settles his feet, if onside pressure occurs from the outside, never try to go around the pressure (which is a common mistake by inexperienced QB's)............ Simply, go *backside*.

Usually a defensive end is pursuing from the backside. One of our offensive linemen is assigned to block this defender. He has an OPTION block on this defender. Which means he will block him the way he wants to go, but further.

Now....if our QB has to go backside, he can read the block of the offensive lineman and go opposite.

In 1987 I had a great QB at Rahway High School in New Jersey by the name of Carols Garay who use to have a field day *going backside*. Carlos went onto a great career at Hofstra University under their great Coach, Joe Gardi.

THE OFF-TACKLE HOLE

Woody Hayes, Ohio State, said that " the off-tackle hole is the most vulnerable hole for the defense to DEFEND." The defensive end or outside linebacker is coached to...."don't open the gates too far and contain the wide running play." WOW!!!!....this is the toughest spot to play on defense.

Don't OPEN THE GATES....and CONTAIN. Well!!!!... what is too tight and what is too wide????? This is the toughest assignment on the defensive front! Coach Hayes said that almost always...you can gain a yard here when you need it.

In Possession Evaluation, I have seen many a team on a short yardage situation, try to hit up in the A or B gap instead of attacking the C gap (the off-tackle hole)....and they come up empty.

Defenses are suppose to be designed to defend from the inside-out.... especially in short yardage situations. Protect the A gap first. Then the B gap...etc. So it is logical to see that the A and B gaps are loaded to stop the Sneak or the quick hitter on short yardage situations.

The off-tackle hole is where to GO. Even if the opponent is guessing you are going there. They STILL have to stop you at the MOST VULNURABLE HOLE. Remember how difficult it is for the defensive player to defend the C gap...

DON'T OPEN THE GATES TOO FAR.....AND CONTAIN.

DOWN AND DISTANCE

Move the chains! Move the chains! Move the chains! So often we have heard this expression.

The coaching legends of the game taught coaches to move the ball forward....... North and South(so to speak). Our other choice is East and West. Where is the goal line? ...... Straight ahead my friend!

Watching college and professional games on TV, I have seen over and over again, teams while in the 4 down zone, start off with a dropback pass on first down (incomplete pass)

....then run on 2nd and 10 for 7 yards only to have a missed 3rd down conversion. Then they have to punt on fourth down or try a field goal

What a missed opportunity!!!!!!!

Maybe they should have run for 7 yards on first down and then have a 2nd and 3 situation!. What do you think????

If they were going to pass on first down in this situation, why not use *play action* with the goal of attacking the defenders that have the two responsibilities of run and pass?

Why show pass *right now* as in the dropback situation and make it easier for defenders to get into their pass cover?

Defenders with run and pass responsibility are taught that they usually must respect the run first. The play fake should hold these defenders and make pass coverage more difficult.

The following is an example of poor play selection and the DESTRUCTION of an Offensive Possession?

A couple of years ago I am watching an NFL game on TV. Team A is winning 6-0 by virtue of two field goals. It is the 3rd period. Team A has the ball on their own 40 yard line. The situation is 3rd and 1. A first down here will give Team A continued possession of the ball and a chance to cross the 50 yard line and get into the 4 down zone. They may continue down for a TD or at least have a chance for a field goal to up their lead. Team B would need 2 scores to catch up. Team A decided to use an end around play on 3rd and 1. They lost 8 yards on the play and had to punt. They ended up losing the game in the fourth quarter.

Play selection lost the game...NOT the players. An end around.....a super delayed play...WOW! How much does that coach get paid?

Every coach I talk to suggests some type of a play going direct. Most coaches say go off tackle with your best back behind your best blocker. A concept I first heard the legend.... Bobby Dodd of Georgia Tech stress.

More games are lost than won!

<u>3RD DOWN CONVERSIONS</u>

Every coach in America knows that success on 3rd down conversions is a major key to winning football games. Thus,it is very important when evaluating offensive possessions to find out why a play succeeded or failed on this important aspect of the game.....*3rd Down Conversions!*

If a pass play is called, the coach calling offense MUST put the QB in a position where he has the best chance for success.

Pass plays with BIG WINDOWS gives the QB a better chance of success rather than patterns with SMALL WINDOWS. Add to this the pattern must be long enough to make the first down after the catch by the receiver.

STOPPING patterns have a higher percentage possibility for the QB rather than MOVING PATTERNS. Right about now, you should be saying to yourself, "yea....but we can't always use STOPPING PATTERNS."

I agree.

What I am saying is that if at all possible, these types of STOPPING patterns …curls….hooks….comebacks, etc. are best.

The proper use of formations can force the defense into single coverage and thus increase the possibility of a pass completion.

On these important *3rd Down Conversion* attempts, screens and draws are also a possibility. Although a well prepared defense is EXPECTING screens and draws.

SCREENS AND DRAWS-

The WORST time to screen or draw is on a long yardage situation. The whole world is waiting for the screen or draw. Your opponent is expecting it. The fans are expecting it. The radio or TV announcers are expecting it.

The BEST time to run a screen or draw in on first down or on a FREE down.

A FREE down could be…2nd and short in the 3 or 4 down zone……3rd and short in the 4 down zone…1st and 10 in any zone.

There are two types of *screens. Quick Screens* and *Slow Screens. Quick Screens* are usually done to the outside and have a better chance to complete.

Slow Screens usually occur over the middle or the interior, tackle to tackle. They are slower and more difficult to execute. Defensive lineman can get in the way. A batted pass is more likely on these screens than on a *Quick Screen*. Thus, if a screen is called on a *3ʳᵈ Down Conversion* attempt, INVEST in a better percentage screen and use a QUICK SCREEN.

I only like *Slow Screens* in one of two situations. On a FREE down or when everything else fails and the need to gamble becomes a choice. *Slow Screens* require perfect timing….more so than *Quick Screens.*

Before these screens are used in a game, they must be perfected in practice and executed 100% perfect. Anything less and you are committing suicide if the play is used in a game.

Thus, *3ʳᵈ Down Conversion* time, is to a large extent, in the hands of the coach calling offense. INVEST in higher percentage possibilities or the coach, rather than the player may be the reason for a failed conversion attempt on 3rd down and a DESTROYED POSSESSION.

RUN DOWN VS. PASS DOWN

There are times during a game when it is obvious that it is a *run down situation* or it is an obvious *pass down situation.* BUT…a team must have in it's offensive game plan, the possibility to …*pass when maybe it should run…..run when maybe it should pass.*

A short selection of plays that the offensive coordinator will call….or a short list of audible calls for the QB in each of the situations mentioned, will give the offense a STRONGER chance of success.

Reading the defense….taking advantage of the weakness of the defensive alignment or coverage….attacking those weaknesses...is an ability that the offense has to have or THEY ARE NOT PREPARED TO WIN!

I enjoy retelling this example;

In 1998 I was the head coach at Madison High School in Madison, New Jersey. We were playing in the State Championship game vs. New Providence High. We had a situation where we were on NPHS's 40 yard line and it was 3rd and 33 yards for a first down.

What do I do now??????

I used a formation where I anticipated the defensive alignment and coverage. The coverage was as expected. They played deep since we needed 33 yards for a first down. The defensive front lined up in their 43 defense as we expected.

We lined up with two wide receivers to each side and a lone back in the backfield...the fullback. We took wide line splits and forced the defensive ends wide.

Instead of running a midline trap, we ran what looked like a midline trap (to hold the middle linebacker) and we long trapped their left defensive end who opened the gates by going with our wide line split.

The attempt here, was to try and get the ball to our small, quick fullback into the spacious defensive secondary (they were deep anticipating pass because we needed 33 yards for a first down)......where our quick fullback could take advantage of his quickness and speed.

Our fullback(on this quick hitter) got into the 2nd level of the defense and was wide open to run. He gained 32 yards before he was tackled.

We then had a 4th and 1 for a first down. We proceeded to attack the off-tackle hole just as Woody Hayes suggested. Our running back barreled through the off tackle hole for a 6 yard gain and a TD.

We Won the State Championship.

We ran the ball....when maybe we should or could have passed the football.

HASH MARKS

The football field is 53 yards and one foot wide. In the high school and college game the hash marks are 18 yards in from the sideline. This means that on the wide side of the field there are 35 yards and 1 foot (we usually just say 36 yards) that the defense has to defend and only 18 yards to the boundary.

Hash Marks can and should be a factor in play selection based on the defense's alignment.

With proper use of offensive formation, the offense can help to dictate the defensive alignment.

By reading the defensive alignment, the QB can tell if the defense is balanced or over-loaded to the wide side of the field or the boundary.

To take advantage of the defensive alignment, an audible system must be available for the QB to use.

In Possession Evaluation, we can evaluate if we as a team took advantage of defensive alignment.

Many times, I have seen the offense RUN INTO THE TEETH OF THE DEFENSE. The defense had more defenders at the point of attack than there were offensive blockers.

HOW CAN THE PLAY SUCCEED?

Failure is guaranteed. It happens over and over again.

- Either the QB was never taught to read defenses…

- …..or the QB missed the read…

- …..or an audible system was not in use.

AGAIN….this is something that we have *control over.* MORE GAMES ARE LOST THAN WON!

In play selection, for every possession, many factors are taken into consideration.

Coaches must take into consideration…

- ….the zones on the field (3 or 4 down zone)…

- ….Coming out zone….Freedom zone….Scoring zone …

- ….Down and distance…

- ….hash mark…

- ….the score…

- ….the weather…

- ….time left in half or game…

- ….injuries…

- ….substitutions…

- ….plays that are doing well.

AUDIBLE SYSTEM

Some coaches stay away from an audible system because they believe it is too difficult for high school kids and a screw up in the audible system will result in a BREAKDOWN.

I do not believe that this statement is correct. I have used an audible system every year I was a head coach (42 years).

I was a head coach on the junior high school level for 3 years and we used an audible system. We used a simple system with just a few choices. We did not make it so complex that we couldn't accomplish our goals.

The lack of an Audible System will cause an offense to BREAKDOWN and destroy a possession quicker than anything.

The QB must have the ability to change a play.

I already mentioned….if the defense is over-load to one side and the offense is going to that side, there are not enough blockers to block all of the defenders. I have seen many games where the offense ran into the teeth of the defense, so to speak.

This is poor coaching.

Usually players get the blame for the unsuccessful play when the coach is the real villain.

We teach our QB's to read the defense from the left to the right….... ALWAYS.

Never change to right to left. Never give away in which direction or location we are going. Be consistent in reading the defense….ALWAYS…left to right.

We teach our defense in their pre-snap reads to read the eyes of opposing QBs and I assume our opponents do the same.

We teach our offensive unit to consider EVERY PLAY TO BE AN AUDIBLE. We do not want our players to be surprised by an audible EVERY PLAY IS AN AUDIBLE is the Mind Set we teach.

We use three different types of audible possibilities;

1. We use a LIVE color. The first number after the LIVE color is the new play.

2. We use a name or a color which designates a *specific* play in our Audible system.

3. We use the word OKIE. If we called an off-tackle play to the right and our opponent's defense was loaded to that side, we call OKIE and run the same off-tackle play but to the left where the defense is balanced with us or undermaned.

On all AUDIBLES we snap the ball on the first number.

In practice we REP…..AND REP…AND REP… AUDIBLES…..over and over…..and over.

In Possession evaluation…..we ask the question…should our QB have used an audible? Did he audible to the correct play?

READING DEFENSES-

Teaching QBs to read defenses is easy.

When I was coaching in Germany, my QB was a All American QB on the Division II college level. He was a great athlete and great person. He was taught to read defenses for the passing game but NEVER for the running game. Thus, he and I sat down and had some fun. I taught him how I read the defense for the running game.

We read the defense by starting off with teaching the LOOKS of all possible defenses.

All the 4 man line defenses…..all the 5 man line defenses…all the 6 man line defenses…etc. We cover all the shades etc.

We teach our QBs to count defenders quickly. Defenses will either be balanced or unbalanced. Loaded to one side.

We teach our QB all of our blocking schemes thus he will know if we can block a specific defensive alignment.

Before the snap, he will know if the play should be run. He has a green light to change every play we use.

The one rule I insist on is….if you change the play…..go from a run to a run…..go from a pass to a pass and on some situations he can audible from a pass to a run.

The QB is taught that he is the coach on the field. He has the best view of the defense.

Our QB MUST be able to audible. I WILL NOT COACH OFFENSIVE FOOTBALL WITHOUT MY QB BEING ABLE TO AUDIBLE.

I mentioned previously, some coaches feel that it is too difficult to teach an audible system. They feel that there are too many possibilities for mistakes….BREAKDOWNS.

What is the trade off if we do not have an audible system in place?

The answer is simple….we do not have the possibility of changing the play, and if the play called was going towards an overloaded defense, the play is guaranteed to fail.

I rather teach……coach ….the AUDIBLE SYSTEM.

Here is a story for you.

In 1995, at Plainfield High School in New Jersey, I had a starting QB on the varsity who was ONLY a freshman. He was a special freshman. Six foot 2 and 190 pounds. A great athlete who could run. He threw passes that were like darts for 70 yards. I knew he was going to make me a great coach. His name was Darryl Kennedy. Daryl went on to play at Syracuse and later had a drink of water with the Pittsburgh Steelers and NFL Europe before an injury ended his career.

Early in the season, the second game, we were playing Irvington High. Early in the game we had the ball on offense, on the 6 yard line going in. I called for a Veer Left from our split back formation. The Veer Left was a triple option full read outside veer play. Darryl calls…"OKIE….OKIE…. OKIE". We call this "OKIE" three times so our guys can have time mentally to make sure of assignments. OKIE simply meant we were using the same play called in the huddle but we were going to run the play to the OPPOSITE side. This audible meant that we were going to change from a Veer Left to a Veer Right. The snap number was on one as it always is on all audible plays. The ball was snapped ....Darryl made a great read on the defensive end....pulled the ball and walked into the end zone for a TD.

When he came off the field, I questioned him why he changed the play. He said, " Coach, I read the defense. They had 6 men to the left of the center and only 5 men to the right. So I called OKIE."

Not bad for a freshman playing varsity football in his first season.

"Hey Coach....How do you win?"

You MUST have the ability to audible. This will increase productivity and when you evaluate possessions, you should have better results.

CHECK WITH ME SYSTEM

Like many teams, we also use a CHECK WITH ME system. It has proved to be very effective and a lot of fun for our players.

Only after teaching the QB how to read defenses are we able to use this system.

We spend a great deal of time in the off season teaching our QBs how to read defenses.

In the off season I will sit down with QB candidates at a long Conference type table. I use large "checkers" game pieces to represent offensive and defensive players. I like this system better than the use of a chalkboard or grease board. It is quicker and makes for better interaction with the QB's.

We use these "checkers" pieces with other position players to learn and test assignments. It works especially good with the linemen.

WHY?

Why do we *not* see more DIRECT quick hitters in the NFL and the college game? I am not talking about the Stretch Play.

These DIRECT quick hitters…the handoff….the dive…seem to NOT BE IN VOGUE. BUT..BUT they can be devastating plays against the defense!

Check this out…In the 2005 Playoff Game with the Pittsburgh Steelers vs. the Indianapolis Colts, the Steelers had the ball on the 20 yard line going in. The Steelers had Jerome Bettis line up 2-3 yards deep in the backfield. They gave him a quick handoff right up the A gap. Bettis romped untouched 20 yards for a TD only to have the play brought back because of a off sides penalty by a wide receiver.

The point here is that the DIRECT quick hitter is a great weapon and has been for years.

Why is this type play not used more It is not in VOGUE!!!!!!

The vogue ever since Ricky Sanders made the STRETCH... ZONE play popular, is to have one back line up 7-8 yards deep. As far as I am concerned,this makes it easier for the defensive linemen to come off blocks and make a play. This deep alignment by the running back makes it harder for offensive lineman to sustain blocks.

I know the philosophy of the zone play and it is great. But, when linemen need to use other types of blocks on different types of running plays, DO THEY HAVE ENOUGH REPS IN PRACTICE TO MAKE OTHER TYPES OF BLOCKS TO MAKE DIFFERENT TYPE RUNS PLAYS WORK? (I watch the NFL every Sunday and Monday and I can tell you that for more than 3 years I never saw a trap play.)

This deep alignment by the one offensive back lets the linebackers line up deeper and it allows them to attack the offensive line of scrimmage DOWNHILL....at better angles.

This type offensive formation also allows the linebackers to line up deeper and it makes it easier for them to get depth in pass coverage.

When a offensive back lines up 3-4 yards deep, in the quick hitter alignment, it forces the linebackers to play closer to the line of scrimmage. Now, the linebackers can not get back as deep or as quick in pass defense as they can when the one back is 7 yards deep.

Another advantage of having the running backs set at 3-4 yards is in the PLAY ACTION PASSING GAME. Fakes are sooner.....linebackers have to be closer to the line of scrimmage, thus....receivers have more open space to negotiate their patterns behind the linebackers.

This type of strategy...the dive..... worked for years.

Why not now?

Because ....this is the modern day and we can not be old fashion. We MUST be in vogue and go along with the crowd. Can you tell I am being facetious?

Bud Wilkinson of Oklahoma fame, taught us with his Split –T offense, that in the DIVE the linemen only have to screen block.....they do not need to hold their blocks very long. It is a tough play to defend. It is VERY QUICK.

One-two-three yards gained are guaranteed. The defense has to make the tackle.

How many times have you seen the defensive player slip off his tackle on these type run plays? Well, in my 47 years of coaching, I have seen it happen more often than not. What seems like a short gain, many times adds up to a 9-10 yard or more gain. Add the fact that a DIRECT play with a broken tackle resulting in a great gain for the offense, is a TREMENDOUS PSYCHOLOCIAL WEAPON.

I can tell you that I as a coach standing on the sideline, I do not like it when my opponent takes the ball and shoves it down our throat....quickly on a handoff. It makes you feel like, "what do we do??? "how do we stop this thing?".

I hear so often TV announcers say that a specific team has....no running game. I notice that the team has NO RUNNING game because of what they are trying to do in the RUNNING GAME.

In my opinion, coaches make it harder for their offensive line and easier for the defensive line and linebackers by the *type of plays* they are *trying to use*....*when* they are trying to use them...and *where on the field* they are trying to use them.

The handoff....the DIRECT quick hitter MUST BE IN YOUR OFFENSIVE RUN PACKAGE..........NO... AND'S... IF'S........ OR BUT'S.

ONE MAN PATTERN-

Years ago, in the 1970's.....I was head coach at Plainfield High School in Plainfield, New Jersey. On Thanksgiving Day we played our arch rival, the Westfield Blue Devils. They had a great coach in Gary Kehler. He built a dynasty program at Westfield. On one of those Thanksgiving mornings we played at Westfield on a muddy field. We were winning 6-0 late into the 4th period. Westfield was primarily a running team and would pass only 4-5 times a game. In this particular situation, Westfield decided to pass the football using only a one man pattern. We rushed the QB....putting on great pressure but they had the house back there blocking. Their one man pattern was a simple hitch pattern to a flanker split way out wide. Our defensive back slipped in the mud and fell to the ground. The receiver caught the ball....scooted by our defensive back 15 yards for the score. They kicked the extra point and we end up losing 7-6.

At the end of the game, I walked across the field and jokingly said to Coach Kehler. " That wasn't fair Gary....only a one man pattern!!!!!!!!!!." He said to me, " Theo......we are only going to throw to one man."

Boy…was he right. I learned a lesson that day.

Would the NFL or a College team use a one man pattern?????
…… I don't think soooo!!!!!!

<u>OTHER POSSESSION
EVALUATION CONSIDERATIONS</u>

- Did we call the correct plays based on the score and the amount of points we needed?

- Did we take into consideration the weather and how it may affect a play called?

- Did we use the clock properly? Did we use our timeouts wisely?

- Did we take advantage of injuries by our opponent and attack their substitutes?

- Did we remember that injuries to one or more of our key players had an affect on our potential offensive or defensive success?

- Did we remember to come back to plays that were successful earlier in the game…or plays that have been successful in past games?

It is here…..Possession Evaluation where we must evaluate our game plan. If we did not take into consider some of the possibilities mentioned above, then we had a *Coaching Breakdown.* We helped to stop ourselves.

Did we have an alternate game plan??????????

Remember a game plan is only good if we are ahead. What do we do with our game plan if we are losing???? Good coaching means that we need to have *alternate game plans. We must be able to make adjustments.*

"HAVE A PLAN FOR EVERYTHING."

Bear Bryant said…. "Have a plan for everything."

An alternate game plan….

- if we are losing by 6 or 7 points…

- if we are losing by 8-9-10 etc.,points

- an alternate game plan when time is a factor.

This is a key question and we better have several answers or we will never be able to make productive adjustments during a game that will help us win.

All these factors are taken into consideration when evaluating the 10 Possession rule.

Remember……we all want to win. "Hey Coach…..How do you win?"

More games are lost than won.

Use the 10 possession rule and EVALUATE your possessions and you will find out that you will have a better chance to win MORE.

DEFENSE

I mentioned earlier that most of this book was going to be on Offensive Breakdowns since it appears…key word APPEARS ….that most Coaching Breakdowns have to do with Play Selection on the offensive side of the ball.

But, I would like to mention a few thoughts about possible Coaching Considerations on the defensive side of the ball.

Factors in evaluating our DEFENSIVE POSSESSIONS!

Were we in proper defensive alignment?

RULE #1 ALIGNMENT

Rule #1 on defense.

In order to play proper defense, Bobby Dodd, Georgia Tech, taught us that *you had to be in proper defensive alignment in order to play proper defense.*

Defenses are developed from the inside-out. Control the A gap …then the B gap etc.

In Possession Evaluation we must evaluate alignment for the defensive front as well as the defensive secondary. Being out of position will help the offensive team to be successful. THIS IS SOMETHING THAT WE CONTROL.

This improper alignment is a BREAKDOWN…a mental error. SOMETHING THAT WE CONTROL.

MORE GAMES ARE LOST THAN WON.

RULE #2 SECONDARY COVERAGE

Rule #2- Was the secondary coverage the BEST call for the situation?

Pre game considerations decide on our GAME PLAN. We must evaluate if our pre-game considerations were correct and if they could have been improved upon.

It is here where we can evaluate secondary personal and whether any players broke down in their specific assignments.

AGAIN....THIS IS SOMETHING WE HAVE CONTROL OVER.

MORE GAMES ARE LOST THAN WON!

Strategically, percentage wise....were we in the coverage that would have given our players the BEST CHANCE TO BE SUCCESSFUL?

Remember....*the coach's responsibility is to put the player in a position to have a chance to be most successful.* Calling the wrong coverage, will put the defensive back in a more disadvantageous situation. This we HAVE CONTROL OVER.

MORE GAMES ARE LOST THAN WON!

RULE #3 PASS RUSH

Rule #3- How about the defensive front?

Did we try to pass rush with only 4 linemen vs. 5 offensive blockers?

Did we help the QB in his passing game by not adding more pressure to the pass rush scheme?

GIVE THE QB….WHAT HE DOESN'T WANT TO SEE

The 2005 NFL playoff game between Indianapolis and Pittsburgh was a great example. The Steelers had their best results when they did NOT allow

Peyton Manning to have time to make correct decisions. They forced quick throws by blitzing strong safety Troy Polamalu and adding outside linebacker pressure with Joey Porter. They went into tight man cover in the secondary. The Steelers had one extra man for the Colts to block and they couldn't do it.

Another great example of pressure.

Back in 1979….the Steelers and their famous STEEL CURTAIN on defense,were playing the Los Angeles Rams in Super Bowl XIV.

Terry Bradshaw was the QB for the Steelers and Vince Ferragamo was the QB for the Rams. All through the game, the Rams tried to get to Bradshaw with only a 4 man rush. The Rams front had great players led by Fred Dryer but they had trouble getting to Bradshaw. He had all day to throw the football. On the other hand, Ferragano spent the day running for his life. The Steelers lined up with 11 men on the line of scrimmage. The Steelers blitzed from everywhere. Ferragamo had limited time to throw the ball.

Needless to say, the Steelers won.

The lesson I learned here......GIVE THE QB....WHAT HE DOESN'T WANT TO SEE .....UNBELIEVABLE PRESSURE.

Pressure where more defenders are rushing as compared to the number of blockers available.

The only way the Rams could have handled the defensive pressure scheme was to add blockers and only send 1 or 2 receivers downfield.....but this would never happen in the pro game.

Remember....any QB would rather have all day to throw. All day to make a correct decision....all day to make a better play. ADD the extra pass rusher and force the QB to make a QUICKER decision. Less time to make a decision means.......*More chance for a bad decision by the QB.*

THE 10 GAME RULE

This is a concept....a RULE that MUST be sold to your team.

In 1949 I was a 12 year old kid living in New York City. My favorite baseball team was the New York Yankees. In those days there were only eight teams in each of the American and National Leagues. They played 154 games a season before the start of the World Series.

In that year, there was a team called the St. Louis Browns who just a couple of years later, left St. Louis for Baltimore to become the Baltimore Orioles.

Well..in those days each team in each league played each other 22 times. Eleven home games and eleven away games. That year, the Yankees beat the Browns 21 times and the Browns only beat the Yankees once. Everyone knew that the Yankees had a better team. After all, they beat the Browns 21-1 in 22 games.

But…..But…..if they only played one game…and it was the one game that the Browns won……what would everyone say? The Browns are better than the Yankees!

Well….we know this not to be true. In later years I always remembered this scenario because in football we usually play a team only once during the season. I remembered the St. Louis browns vs. the New York Yankees. I would use this story with my teams. If we going well and winning and we played a team with a poor record, I would remind my team of how the Yankees lost to the Browns. Thus I established what I called the…..*10 Game Rule.*

By using this rule with my team, I felt I was using the old saying….. *"an ounce of prevention is worth a pound of cure."* Normally, if we were to play an opponent 10 games, maybe we win 5 and they win 5. We would try to sell of our team… …*"let's not have it be one of those 5 losses…let's have it be one of those 5 wins".*

Or maybe we would win 6 of 10…or 7 of 10….again…" let's make it one of those wins and not one of those losses."

If we played a very poor team we would probably win 9 of 10 games. The one loss would be like the time when the St. Louis Browns beat the Yankees back in 1949….once in 22 games. *Let's not have it happen to us…!*

MURPHY'S LAW

…..remember Murphy's Law. *Everything that can go wrong…. does go wrong!!!!*

It can happen. Trust me…it can happen and it has happened to me over the years.

We can be over confident. The newspaper's predictions say we are going to win. Everyone thinks it is going to be an easy game. This is when the favorite or the better team ends up losing the game. On some occasions, you may win the game but play very poorly and just win by a hair. You almost get upset.

Some years ago I took a survey of college games of who were favored to win and the results. On Sunday morning I would tabulate the scores from the local newspaper's sport section. Every week, 20-30 percent of games won were WON by the underdog. When tabulating the Top 25 college teams in the country, 18-25 percent lost to so called inferior teams.

Remember the ole saying, "On any given Sunday"…or Saturday…….or Friday Night!!!!!! The *so called best team* doesn't always win.

In the mid-1980's I served as head coach at Sayreville High School in Sayreville, New Jersey. We anticipated having a great team that year. But injuries really took it's toll on our success early in the season. We started of terrible (as far as the record was concerned)….0-6 …Wow.

In our game seven we played J.P. Stevens High School who was on a roll. They came to our place with a 7-0 record and we were picked to lose badly.

Naturally, we always tried to sell our players the 10 Game Rule and it did not matter whom we played. We could win or we could lose. Well, we won this game 15-13. A big, so called upset.

After the game, the newspaper reporters came up to me and said," Coach how did you do it?" Like I had mirrors or some magic!! I called over one of my players, tight end Matt Fulham and told him to answer the question for the reporters. Matt went onto explain the 10 Game Rule and how we developed the proper Mind Set to be able to compete with anyone with any record. Boy, I was proud of him and of his explanation. This was the teaching of the 10 game Rule and how it paid off.

Flip it around. We have a great record and we are going to play a team that hasn't won a game all season. We as coaches worry about complacency. We worry about our fans not taking this opponent seriously. The same with parents. I've had parents tell me we are going to win EASILY. WOW.... do I worry. You bet your life I worry. It is in situations like this where we really pound home the 10 Game Rule into the heads of our players.

Back in the late 1960's we had a real good team at Sewanhaka High School in Floral Park out on Long Island in New York. We were going to play Lawrence High School in the season opener. The newspapers made their predictions and had us winning big..... 35-0. Wow! I knew we were in trouble. Lawrence always had a good team. They had a great coach in "Black Jack" Martalotta.

To start off the game, we fumbled the kickoff return and they score a touchdown on their first play. After the next kickoff we run one play and lose a fumble and they score a second touchdown to go up 14-0. We return the next kickoff back to mid field and on first down we throw an interception which resulted in another Lawrence TD. With less than 3 minutes into the game we are losing 21-0. One of their players runs by our sideline and shouts to me, " Hey Coach…..read the newspapers?"……

Well…I go up and down the sidelines trying to settle our guys down. I AM TRYING TO SELL them that that we have plenty of time. We can win. We can come back. Guess what the final score was. We lost 21-20. On our last TD we miss the extra point and we lose our ace placekicker when he got hit with a late hit and could not return to the game. The game ended with us marching for another score. The game ended with us on their 35 yard line going in. Too far for a field goal, especially with our kicker knocked out of the game. We ran out of clock.

Remember…..."Hey Coach….How do you win?" *MIND SET….MIND SET….MIND SET…! "But you have to teach it…you have to coach it…"*

"You have to have this concept in your checklist of Things to do!"

More games are lost than won. The 10 Possession rule. The 10 Game rule. Tied together they are the building blocks…. the foundation of every program I tried to build.

Thus, our team learns….we can win any game and we can lose any game…..!

COMMUNICATION

Communication is THE MOST IMPORTANT system that we use.

Communication is THE MOST IMPORTANT system we use on and off the field. It is more important than our offensive system…our defensive system….our kicking game system…..our conditioning system….our off season program. *It is more important than anything we coach.*

Our Communication SYSTEM…works on and off the Field. If you want to win. If you want to *learn how to win.* You have to master this one system…….COMMUNICATION.

Poor communication causes BREAKDOWNS during a game…and remember what Bear Bryant said….. BREAKDOWNS EQUATE TO;

"More games are lost than won"

Remember the 10 Possession Rule. Poor communication can destroy your possessions. Poor communication can cause morale problems on and off the field.

FAIRNESS

At this time I want to talk about *Fairness* and how it affects communication.

I sell our coaches… ".not only is it important to be fair but it is more important to appear to be fair."

Let me repeat that……."not only is it important to be fair but it is more important to appear to be fair."

I had a coach a few years ago that was having a communication problem with one of his position players. I talked with the player and the player told me he thought that the Coach was not being fair. I knew the Coach to be a very fair person and I knew that the player had the wrong perception of the Coach. Regardless….the only thing that counted was that the player thought the Coach was not fair and this was causing a problem for the team.

I spoke with the assistant coach and instructed him to have a one on one meeting with the player and try to correct his perception. He had to have several meetings with the player to make the correction of the perception that his position player had about him.

In order for the position coach to get his players to the next level of performance, the players have to have TRUST in the position coach.

A Player must think that the coach is being fair in order to TRUST the coach. A lack of TRUST in the coach will have a negative affect on the coach's productivity.

In team talks, I try to stress to our players that in truth..... many times,..... *life is not fair.* I try to sell the players that we as a staff try to be as FAIR as we can be. We understand that we need to develop TRUST and TRUST is a two way street between coaches and players. We try to sell the concept that the goal of the player must be TO NOT ALLOW ANY ELEMENT(in this case his perception of fairness) TO STOP HIM FROM SUCCESS.

Sometimes this is a tough sell but a player will make himself stronger mentally if he can accomplish this goal.

"DO NOT ALLOW THE ELEMENTS TO AFFECT YOUR PERFORMANCE IN A NEGATIVE WAY!"

We know that to win a game is tough. We not only have to overcome our opponent....but we have to overcome the officials...plus the weather...plus the bounces etc. It is tough enough to win a game so it is totally unnecessary to have more of a challenge in winning by having morale problems with players. *This we have control over.* This is one of those factors that we can control.

If you want to destroy your team fast, have a group of players on your team that think you or THE coaches on your staff are not fair. They will lose TRUST in you and your staff. And ....you know how important TRUST IS if you are going to WIN!

I believe that if a player has great TRUST in the coaches.... he will make a bigger COMMITMENT to the program. This I believe.

Lack of communication in the *actual game* of football, can also destroy your team quickly, because of BREAKDOWNS on offense....defense...or kicking game.

Poor communication in the offensive huddle. ...poor communication in defensive calls by the defense.....poor communication in the kicking game can all cause DESTRUCTION and LOSING. Every coach knows this fact. But......it must be on your list of considerations in evaluating staff performance and morale of the team.

TESTING AND COMMUNICATION

Testing and Communication go hand in hand. THUS it is of paramount importance to TEST your players. TEST if communication was CORRECT.

Tests can be ... oral...written or visual.

WRITTEN TESTS

In the past we have had great success giving written tests. They should be short and not too long of an assignment.

When we have the players first take a test, we have the players TAKE HOME the test and use their playbooks. This is an OPEN BOOK TAKE HOME EXAM. They had better get the correct answers…. especially when you consider they can use their playbooks.

When the player returns the test, we usually have the position coach GRADE one exam and then assign a position player to correct all the exams of fellow position players. This gives the player additional REPS and learning becomes reinforced.

Then the position coach checks the tests before he returns them to his position players to double check for correctness and to evaluate player performance on the test.

The next time we give this SAME test, we have the players take the test under the supervision of the position coach in a classroom setting. No help here! No open book! No take home test!…Now we will see if they really know their stuff!!!!!

The position coach will correct one test and then as before, a position player will correct the rest of the tests of players playing his position. It really makes for great learning.

Once the tests have been graded, the position coach reviews all errors and hands the tests back to the players for review.

ORAL TESTS

Oral tests are easy and can be fun. I use a teaching technique I developed years ago in the classroom setting.

When I ask a question and expect an answer from a player, I insist that the player give the answer immediately and *not have to stop and think for the answer.* I tell our players, "you have to know the answer like you know your name."

For example......I ask a player....What is your name? The player responds quickly with his name. He doesn't HAVE to think about it. He knows his name. Then I ask a very difficult question. The player hesitates....I say WRONG! The player usually laughs because I didn't give him time to think of the answer to the question.

Well....I sell our players that if you have to hesitate, then you do not know the answer. To hesitate and then answer..... is not good enough. You have to know the answer like you know your own name.

When a play is called in the huddle, the player can not think about his assignment. He must know it .... INSTANTANEOUSLY.

If an audible is called at the line......he can not think...HE HAS TO KNOW WHAT TO DO INSTANTANEOUSLY.

VISUAL TESTS

We have had great success and fun with a visual test that I developed some years ago. I use the pieces that are used in the game of checkers to represent 11 men on offense and 11 men on defense. We work with all position players with this visual type test.

With the offensive linemen we REP and test blocking assignments. We REP and test the defensive front about defensive alignments and stunts and linebacker coverages. We take our defensive secondary and test them on their coverages. We take our receivers and test them on their patterns and the Hot Receiver system that we use.

And most important of all…..we take our Quarterbacks and teach them how to read defenses….both for the passing game and the running game.

This is an outstanding teaching aid as well as TESTING aid. This visual teaching and testing technique helps in our COMMUNICATION SYSTEM so we can eliminate BREAKDOWNS ……because we know;

MORE GAMES ARE LOST THAN WON…..and we know THE 10 POSSESSION RULE.

Finally, great communication comes with the learning of PEOPLE SKILLS.

I will discuss this in detail with the writing of my next book.. Positive Mind Set….Special Mind Set.

EVERYTHING IS FOR A REASON!

In our Communication to our team…..we sell our team on the concept….. "everything is for a reason" Everything we do on and off the field is for a reason. A player must TRUST us as coaches.

Whatever we try to teach as skills is for a GOOD reason. Whatever rules we have for the team are for a GOOD reason.

In our teaching (Coaching),we usually try to explain …WHY…we do something. This helps to sell the player on the importance of why we are doing what we do. We try to SELL AND NOT TELL. All the skills we teach…….all the X's and O's we teach….are for a REASON. We encourage our players to ask questions regarding what we teach.

When a player asks a question, rather than simply answering the question, I try to get the player to answer his own question by saying…."it must be for a reason"….TELL ME WHY? I try to get the player to think. I use leading statements (hints) to try to get the player to come up with the answer to his own question. This INTERACTION technique is better than I simply answering the question. Using this technique, I try to get the player to use his brain.

Obviously, this technique is done during a meeting situation NOT on the practice field or during game time. This is a technique of " selling….not telling". This is very important if we expect the player to believe in what he is doing.

This helps to accomplish the things we have already mentioned;

- Get the player to the next level of performance.

- Eliminate BREAKDOWNS

- Increase team productivity.

WHAT IS YOUR GOAL?

And finally....under communication...we try to sell our players that they must always know......WHAT IS YOUR GOAL? Knowing what your goal is, always helps the player create that sense of urgency which helps concentration during learning. Knowing what your goal is, helps to improve communication. Our #1 Goal is to WIN! Breakdowns will cause us to not reach our goal....to WIN!

Breakdowns are caused many times by poor communication on or off the field. With poor communication we do not reach our #1 goal which is to WIN!

We communicate to our players FOOTBALL GOALS.... on and off the Field Goals. Goals about football and Goals about their personal lives.

Goals in the Present and Goals for the Future. Individual goals and team goals.

We teach that for every goal.....we must have a solution to reach that goal. In other words....a Plan...as was mentioned before by Bear Bryant (a Plan for Everything). A Goal without a Plan to accomplish the Goal is worthless.

As I mentioned at the beginning of this segment...... Communication is our #1 System.......Communication is our Most Important System.

"Hey Coach......how do you win????"

Communication .....Gentlemen............ Communication...!

FADS... BEING IN VOGUE!

Coaches, like people, LOVE the FADS of the day. Coaches, like people, like to be in vogue. What is the fashion of the day?

I dare say that many a coach HAVE lost football games because they wanted to be in vogue. They wanted to be in style. They did not want to be considered old FASHIONED.

In 1971, at the National Football Clinic in Atlantic City, New Jersey...I heard Darryl Royal speak. As head coach of the University of Texas, they were the 1970 National Champions and the Longhorns were riding the offensive rage of the day....the ole mighty WISHBONE offense.

At the clinic were coaches from all over the country(over 2500 in attendance). When they went home, many of them installed the Wishbone.

Some were lucky to win but many found out the Wishbone was not for their team and personnel. But, the Wishbone was the FAD of the day....it was in VOGUE.

During that Clinic, Coach Royal said something that I have lectured on ever since. I heard him say ...... *"Gentlemen....... you DO NOT want my offense......you want my fullback."* WOW!

Remember......*PLAYERS WIN* not offenses.

For fear of being called "old fashion", many a coach changes his offense almost every year or when a new offensive FAD comes along. Even worse......some coaches "change horses in mid-stream"....change their offensive or defensive system in the middle of the season.

Every year there seems to be a new offense or defense in vogue. Every year there are NEW words for OLD words. Coaches copy new offenses NOT because they are good for their players but because they are NEW.

Coaches like to be UP TO DATE.

Coaches spend a tremendous amount of time during their career learning all there is to know about certain offenses or defenses. They get REPS in learning. They can BEST teach what they know. Then they decide to do something NEW because it is the rage of the day. Change horses and you have to learn all over again.

I am not saying that you have to be stagnant. But to change for the sake of being in vogue is foolish. Chances are, the coach always trying to be in vogue doesn't even know he is doing that. He might sell himself that he is trying to be intricate and deceptive. What he is really doing is LOSING all the time he spent on REPS ......learning and mastering a specific offense or defense. The coach went through great pain to learn so that HE COULD BE A GREAT TEACHER of his system. He teaches his players a system so *they* will not BREAKDOWN. Key word here..is ……………*they*!

They would not breakdown. Then the coach jumps to a new different offense.

The BEST offense or defense is the offense or defense that can be BEST TAUGHT….regardless of what it is. As long as the offense or defense is SOUND.

HOW AND WHEN

All offensive and defensive systems that have been developed through the years are sound. Thus, they are all GOOD.

You can argue that one is better than the other, BUT, I suggest that more important than what system is better, HOW we use the system and WHEN do we use the system is MORE important. How does the system fit your personnel? That is the most important reason for using any system!

DEVELOPMENT OF OFFENSES AND DEFENSES

Going back to the early days of football, football was primitive as compared to today.

As the years went by, Offenses were developed and then Defenses were developed to counter and stop the new Offenses. Then the Offense would continue development to overtake the weakness of the newly developed Defenses.

Then the Defense would find out how to control the new Offense. And so on, and so on!

Through the years, we have learned that every defense has it's weaknesses.

Offensive coaches try to exploit these weaknesses. There can be as many as 10 gaps for the defense to cover on the *First Level* …the line of scrimmage.

The *Second Level*…coaches usually divide this area into 5 zones…2 flats areas and 3 hook areas.

The *Third Level* of defense can be divided into 3 -4- or 5 zones.

Regardless, there are more areas for the defense to defend than there are players.

The challenge for the offense is to try and find an open area and exploit that open area…a weakness.

The 4-3 defense was first developed to stop the great passing game of professional football. The 4-3 defense was *not* designed to stop the Wing-T offense.

Today, when a 4-3 defense has to play a Wing-T offense, many adjustments have to be made by the defense in alignment, reads, assignments. The 2 inside defensive tackles are usually asked to "get up field". This technique sets up the defense to get hurt with the mid-line trap over center….the ole fashion Buck Trap. THUS…..adjustments in assignment by the 2 inside tackles MUST be made by the defense or the defensive system will be responsible for the defense getting beat on this type of offensive play.

Back in 1993, one of my friends was coaching one of the local colleges in New Jersey. They were using the 4-3 defense and they had a difficult time with an opponent early in the year that was using the Wing-T. In this game, the opponent's fullback had 208 yards on the ground using the Buck Trap.

WHY? Because the defensive tackles were not taught trap reaction vs. a Wing-T type offense. The inside tackles would continue to "get up field" all game and their opponent trapped them out of the Stadium.

Was this a case of player failure? ….or Coach failure?

It was great play selection by the offensive coordinator of their opponent.

It was poor defensive preparation by the defensive coaches.

Remember…. *"More games are lost than won!"*

REMEMBER WHY THE SYSTEM WAS DEVELOPED!

When a coach is learning the game of football he is a *Student of the Game.* He should learn why specific defenses were designed. This information gives the coach knowledge of *How to Attack Specific Defenses.* Systems are developed for a reason…Remember the concept……IT MUST BE FOR A REASON …

Every offense was designed to defeat a specific defense. Every Defense was designed to stop a specific offense....thus the reason for the concept of using a MULTIPLE Offense and a MULTIPLE Defense.

NO SUCH THING

The is NO SUCH THING as an offensive coach or a defensive coach.

How can a coach be great at offense if he doesn't understand everything about defenses? How can a coach be a great defensive coach if he doesn't know everything about offenses?

I remember Tom Landry being interviewed on TV when he first took over the Dallas Cowboys. The reporter asked Landry.....and I am paraphrasing, "Coach....you were a defensive coordinator....and now you bring all these new offensive trends to the Cowboys (Dallas shift....multiple formations...extensive use of motion)......How come?.....you were a defensive coach." Coach Landry simply explained that as a defensive coordinator he had to learn everything about offense and he decided that when he became a head coach he would use the offensive schemes that he felt were most troublesome for his defensive units in the past.

The message here is that as a *Student of the Game*.....we as coaches must be an expert in all phases of the game. NEVER be considered an OFFENSIVE or DEFENSIVE Coach. We need to learn EVERYTHING and become a MASTER Coach at everything.

THE BEST

The BEST system is MULTIPLE. Multiple Offense and Multiple Defense.

MULTIPLE OFFENSE

Multiple Offense with plays from all categories of plays…run and pass..

Direct, delayed and special……include the option package of speed options, counter speed option, double and triple options and trap options.

Multiple offense does NOT mean that I am suggesting you use a GRAB BAG offense. A GRAB BAG offense is a term used to describe offensive play selection which appears to be plays selected for no rhyme or reason.

Multiple means that we have to have the ability to use different types of plays and formations to take advantage of a specific defense's weakness. In this way…..when developing our game plan or when we make adjustments during a game, we have the ability to give our offense ….our players the best chance to be successful.

Remember the concept……*A coach's responsibility is to put his players in the best position to be successful.* This is what GREAT coaching should do.

I do NOT believe, as do some coaches, that to run the option, the option has to be your bread and butter. These coaches believe that you have to coach option and nothing but option. *I do not believe this and never have. Through the years I have proved that you can run the option package successfully and have a Multiple Offense loaded with all the other categories of plays.* It comes down to REPS and teaching. YOU CAN DO IT! It comes down to what you believe. I BELIEVE!

The passing game must include all possibilities. Three step and five step drop.....play action....sprintouts.....bootlegs....... screens and draws. A great 2 minute package must be in use. This 2 Minute Offense must be practiced....REPS....and be made to be used anytime, not just with 2 minutes left in the game.

Being MULTIPLE helps the offense have a better chance to make better adjustments during a game. As a coach you do not want to BREAKDOWN a possession because of a lack of the ability to take advantage of a weakness in the opponents defensive scheme.

NOW!.....BEING MULTIPLE.... THE COACH WILL ALWAYS BE IN VOGUE!

MULTIPLE DEFENSE

Multiple Defense with all possibilities of adjustments is a *must*.

Sixty-seven years ago, teams would use one set defense and never use a defensive huddle. When the offensive team broke their huddle and came up on the ball, the defense simply LINED up. No defensive call......no stunts.....just LINE UP. Eventually, the defensive huddle came into being and calls were made to change coverages, fronts, alignments etc.

When I started coaching in 1959 I used the 60 defense that I learned in college and from studying the defense used by Coach Bear Bryant. Coach Bryant believed that for every offensive play called, the defense should also call a play of their own. He stressed that the defense is NEVER DEFENDING. The defense is always on the OFFENSE. Since there are more ways to score on defense than offense, this concept made sense. Thus, we taught our teams........*"we are always on offense".*

The "Bear" believed that you should attack the offense on every play and not sit back and let them attack you. Thus, 95% of the time my teams were in a PRESSURE defensive front of some type.

Our base defense over the past 12 years was the 35 defense. But, we adjusted out of this defense to all variations of the 33.....34......

35....44.....43.....all the   60's..etc. We had several pass covers. We used a multitude of pass rush schemes. *BUT ALWAYS.....we were ATTACKING!*

MULTIPLE OFFENSE   and   MULTIPLE DEFENSE enabled us to *always be able* to make adjustments during the game and during halftime.

BY BEING MULTIPLE...WE WERE ALWAYS IN VOGUE!

PLAYERS WIN!

Vince Lombardi said over and over again......*PLAYERS WIN*. Ole Vince said we do not coach football …..we coach people. People are players and players win. NOT COACHES. Yes, coaches help to win but without great or good players, a coach will never win. Players do the blocking and players do the tackling…..not Coaches. Players are why we recruit…. why we draft…..why players are traded… …why one player makes more money than another player.

A coach's responsibility is TWO fold;

1. Help the player move to the next level of performance…. increase his productivity. Using a scale of A-B-C-D….. if you have a C player, your goal as a coach is to get that player to become a C+or a B or even higher. If your team is made up of all C players and you play a team of all A players. Guess who is going to win most of the time?

2. Put a player in the best position to be successful. A coach must ask a player to do what he is mentally and physically

prepared and able to do. If a coach asks a player to do a skill or run a play or defense that the player has limited skill or readiness to do, then the possibility of the player being successful is limited and the chances of failure are greater and the chance for success is less.

This is a great example;

- A quarterback has a 3rd down conversion situation facing him.

- His coach sends in a pass play.

- Does the play give the QB the best chance to be successful?

- Does the pattern called have a designed BIG WINDOW or a SMALL WINDOW.

- If the coach called for a BIG WINDOW, he gave the QB a better chance to be successful. A SMALL WINDOW would limit the success possibility of the QB since a BIG WINDOW is always better than a SMALL WINDOW.

- If the pass called has a SMALL WINDOW and the QB fails to make the 3rd down conversion, fails to complete the pass ….many fans, media etc., will say the QB did not get the job done. *The real culprit was the coach who called the play and gave the QB a lesser chance for success.*

Do you remember.?….MORE GAMES ARE LOST THAN WON… …the 10 Possession rule?……this was an example of poor coaching.

Gentlemen….if you do these two things…Help the player to increase his level of play….and….put your players in the best position to be successful…..you are a great coach.

GREAT COMMUNICATION MAKES FOR BETTER PLAYERS

Great people skills will help a coach communicate better with his players. Thus the players will have a better chance to learn more and faster and thus have a better chance to move to the next level of productivity…next level of performance. *Players Win* when there is great communication.

FUN HELPS PLAYERS WIN!

Duffy Daugherty, the legendary coach from Michigan State University stressed in his coaching, " you gotta make it *FUN.* If it is not *FUN.* then it is not worth doin'" *FUN* will make the player's experience on the team more rewarding and increase the player's desire to want to be on the team…. *FUN* helps a player to be more coachable…. …

FUN helps PLAYERS WIN!.

On our locker-room bulletin board, we list our Team Goals for the Season. The #1 Goal is always; *FUN*

I have heard some college coaches, who give scholarships, and some professional Coaches, say; "Forget about fun…they are getting paid…this is a business." I believe that this attitude is a lot of crap…period! Everyone who goes to work likes to enjoy their job, their WORK. If it is FUN, productivity is always higher.

Soooooooooo………make it FUN and your chances of WINNING are better!

In 1983 I was the head coach at St. Thomas Aquinas High School in North Edison, New Jersey. We Won our Conference Championship and went to the State Playoffs. We won the first round. In the Championship game we played St. John Vianny. We were winning 3-0 on a field goal we converted in the first half. With one minute and 10 seconds left in the game, they threw a Hail Mary pass to their top receiver who was double covered by two of our defensive backs. The pass deflected off one of our defenders into the hands of the St. John Vianny receiver for a TD. We lost the game 7-3. This was not FUN. Losing is NEVER FUN.

In the off-season, I left St. Thomas (later to be called Bishop Ahr HS) to rebuild another program and Coach Tony Aschettino took over as head coach. He went on to continue the winning way and win several State Championships. One of the local newspapers….the News tribune…. wrote a big article about the GREEK. It was a great article about my coaching travels and accomplishments. In the article Coach Aschettino was quoted saying, "every Coach in America should coach one year with Coach Theo……what you learn and the FUN you have is unbelievable." This statement was one of the finest compliments that I ever received.

Tony said……it was FUN. It was FUN. It was FUN.

Hey Coach.......How do you win?...Make it FUN.....
PLAYERS WIN

FUN AND ENTHUSIASM

Fun and enthusiasm go hand in hand. Back in 1962 I heard Bear Bryant tell a great story about.....*enthusiasm is caught.....not taught.* The Bear-and I am paraphrasing, said; " A man went out into the street. He had a can of gasoline. He took the can of gasoline and poured it over his body. He took a match, lit the match and put himself on FIRE. Everyone came out of their houses. Cars stopped in the road. People started yelling...that man is on FIRE!

That Gentlemen... is a MAN PUTTING HIMSELF ON FIRE. THAT IS HOW ENTHUSIASM WORKS. GO OUT THERE AND GET EXCITED....PUT YOURSELF ON FIRE AND SEE WHAT HAPPENS.....PEOPLE WILL WATCH YOU AND FOLLOW YOU....THEY TOO WILL GET EXCITED.....................

ENTHIUSASM IS CAUGHT....NOT TAUGHT."

I thought this was great story and have used it for years. It is FUN to put yourself on FIRE. It shows enthusiasm.........excitement.

Sometimes we say...GET EXCITED.....FIRE IN THE BELLY.....and PUT YOURSELF ON FIRE...remember...enthusiasm can create FUN ....

ENTHUSIASM IS CAUGHT... NOT TAUGHT!

"There is no ENTHUSIASM around here"-

When and if a coach comes into the office and says, " There is no FIRE around here....no enthusiasm. Everyone is dead." What should the coach do? Who is responsible for enthusiasm in the locker-room or on the field?

The answer is simple. The Coach is ALWAYS responsible for the FIRE. It is during these times, when the team is DEAD, that the coach must put himself on FIRE and CREATE the enthusiasm needed to increase productivity.

This is LEADERSHIP.

Joe Paterno had a great statement....*"When the players get down.........the coaches must get up!"*

OLE JAKE GAITHER... NOT X'S AND O'S

Jake Gaither, the legendary coach from Florida A&M University said back in 1962....

Football is not about X's and O's......Football is about Billy's and Joe's Players Win!

BILL PARCELLS... TEAM FIRST PLAYERS

Bill Parcells...the great NFL coach...said over and over again, "I am looking for..Team-first players...Not...ME-first players." Ole Bill knows that PLAYERS WIN. The best players are not necessarily the best athletes. This is a very important statement. Parcells knows that the best players are TEAM FIRST players...they have that SPECIAL MIND SET that makes for winning.

"3 TEAMS OUT THERE!"

We teach our players, that during a game.....there are 3 teams out there on the field..........

....Them....us and the zebras.......

- we have no control over our opponents and what they try to do!

- we have no control over the officials!

- WE DO HAVE CONTROL OVER WHAT WE DO!

PLAYERS WIN......or Lose......Remember......*More games are lost than won....*

WIN THE OFFICIALS

We sell our team and coaching staff that we must WIN THE OFFICIALS. We have some control over this. Before the game even starts, we have a pre-game meeting with the officials about rules, special plays etc. It is at this time that we try to sell the officials on our coaching mind set. I tell the officials that I am the only coach that is allowed to talk to them. My assistant coaches are taught that their job is to coach their position players and make coaching adjustments and substitutions.

The goal here is to convince the officials that we are SPECIAL. Most coaches spend a lot of time during a game getting into the ear of the officials. We teach our staff that...*we can not coach and officiate at the same time.* There may be an official that has "rabbit ears" and he may be a little quick to throw a flag against us.....especially a unsportsmanlike conduct call against our sideline. We do not want to help our opponents with a dumb move like this. We try to NOT stop ourselves.... a breakdown...a loss of a possession. WE TRY TO TAKE THE OFFICIALS OUT OF THE GAME.

Trust me when I say that as a young coach I was the worst when it came to yelling at the officials. I would get so excited...angry....my head would pound. Then a great friend of mine....Bob Schussler, the head coach at Hempstead High on Long Island died of a heart attack on the sideline. WOW! I said, I better find another way or I am next. I found a BETTER WAY.

A few years ago, I was the head coach of the Luebeck Cougars in the German Football League in Luebeck, Germany and we were playing the Hamburg Blue Devils at our home field. I had my usual talk with the officials before the game. The referee said to me…"We'll see Coach…if you are a man of your word". He had some doubt that I would not be yelling and screaming on the sideline. At the end of the game, the referee came up to me and said…"You are a man of your word". He was use to other coaches yelling constantly during games that he officiated.

FOOTBALL IS ABOUT
BLOCKING AND TACKLING

When I started coaching back in 1959, I was taught that football is about blocking and tackling. In fact…while attending football clinics through the years….coaches always talked about football being about blocking and tackling. Offenses do not work without blocking and defenses are only as good as the tackling that is done by a team using a specific defense.

But, we are ALSO taught that blocking and tackling are 90% desire and 10% technique. If this is true….and I truly believe it is true…..blocking and tackling are ALL ABOUT DESIRE….. Then we should be coaching and teaching desire 90% of the time…

The trouble is, we do not!!!!!!!

We have checklists for all phases of offense. Checklists for defense. Checklists for the kicking game. Checklists for conditioning and other phases of football.......*but do we have a checklist for coaching DESIRE????*

The Question is….when do we coach desire? When do we have time? The other phases of the game take so much time and it seems that there are not enough hours in the day to get it all done. I believe some coaches make a terrible mistake by not making coaching DESIRE a main concern. I have always taken this DESIRE skill as a very important part of coaching, thus years ago I developed what I call………………… our POSITIVE MIND SET PROGRAM. It is with this program that we teach concepts that can help players make themselves stronger people. Stronger people, stronger players mentally……

- can acquire better self-discipline

- can acquire better self-confidence

- can acquire better focus

- can acquire the ability to pay attention to detail better

- can become better Leaders

- can learn how to put themselves on FIRE

- can demonstrate DESIRE

Teaching and coaching DESIRE can be done by the coaching staff during the season and in the off-season. Anytime we come in contact with our players, our demeanor, our attitude, the way we carry ourselves, our communication with our players…..this all helps to create the POSITIVE MIND SET in the player that we are looking for. This POSITIVE MIND SET helps to create DESIRE in the player. This important topic is discussed at length in my book.....*Positive Mind Set....Special Mind Set.*

PLAYERS WIN!

FINDING THEM... IS BETTER THAN MAKING THEM!

Two ideas that have helped me through the years, to FIND players.

TOUCH FOOTBALL GAME

In the off season, beside running our Strength Program, I have used a *Touch Football Game* to evaluate and FIND players for the upcoming season. This was especially great to evaluate NEW players. It also gave me an opportunity to evaluate NEW players vs. the returning vets.

The teams were usually 4 on 4 or 5 on 5. You do not want larger teams because you want them to all get a chance to run, catch and throw. I would just take a chair and sit under a shady tree, if one was available. I would not be involved at all. This way I could evaluate;

- leadership

- ability to run and cut

- ability to catch

- ability to throw

- who will sacrifice their body for the ball

- who was not afraid

- who was aggressive and to what extent

- ability to play man cover

- who would not quit

- what the reaction was to cuts and bruises from diving for the ball and hitting the ground.

I found MANY A PLAYER in these fun games. The NEW players showed me what position they should start at when the season would begin.

BIG MAN (FAT MAN) BASKETBALL

A basketball league for the BIG MEN….the fat boys….was a great help to me through the years. Usually done during the summer at the local playground. The games were made up of 4 on 4 or 3 on 3…..never 5 on 5. The games were played either half court or full court if possible. I wanted the guys to run…..run….run…..and run.

These games helped me to evaluate several of the traits and abilities that I have already mentioned. These game provided great FUN and CONDITIONING.

Basketball is a great game for developing basic athletic skills, thus a by-product of this activity helped the BIG guys to develop their agility and quickness.

Players Win!

PLAYERS WIN DESPITE THE COACH!

Wow….is this true! I wish I had a dollar for every time a player made a coach look good. PLAYERS MAKE PLAYS. Even when the play called could be considered a poor play selection. Players make coaches LOOK GOOD……. including myself. Often I have told the press that a certain player is making me a GREAT coach. It still comes down to talent….PLAYERS.

PLAYERS WIN!

DISCIPLINE

Discipline is not what you do _to someone_........
Discipline is what you do _for someone_.........

Most athletes think that discipline means punishment. It depends on your mind set. It is my opinion and so it is with many other coaches, without great discipline a team will never get to the Championship level of play.

There are three types of discipline that we are concerned with.

1. _Discipline given out by a higher power source_, such as a coach giving discipline to a player. In order for a player to be coachable, the player needs to be able to accept discipline issued out by the coaching staff.

Players have always wanted discipline. Players want to know what they can do and what they can not do. Players want _Direction and Leadership_. A great leader knows how to use discipline in a Positive way. Poorly disciplined teams have no direction….no leadership. Players accept discipline providing the coach has sold his team that he is fair.

2. *Self discipline* is probably the most important type of discipline. A player needs to learn how to have self-discipline. This is hard to do, especially for young players. Self-discipline is a PERSONAL DEVELOPMENT skill that needs to be mastered by any athlete if he ever hopes to reach his potential. Self-discipline allows the athlete to learn how to *pay attention to detail.* Paying attention to detail gives the athlete the ability to FOCUS on the small things and thus increase productivity. Self-discipline allows the athlete the ability to move to the next level of performance. *Players Win* and players with great self-discipline have a great chance to be a Champion.

When we look at the great Champions of all sports, we see people who demonstrate great self-discipline in their practice habits and their daily life habits.

3. *Discipline administered by one's peers*….such as a Captain asserting himself in the heat of battle of a game toward another player. There comes a time when players have to be able to sacrifice their personal feelings for the cause of the team.

REWARD AND PUNISHMENT SYSTEM

I SELL our coaching staff and team on the need for a *Reward and Punishment System.*

REWARD

Rewards are given to our players in the form of *Recognition*. I will mention our recognition system in a later chapter in this book.

When a player is a member of the team in good standing.... we consider this to be a reward. The player earned the privilege of being a team member.

When the player gets a chance to play in a game, this is a reward for being coachable and achieving a certain level of competence.. He earned the right to play.

PUNISHMENT-....

Punishment comes in the form of a specific type of discipline. If you screw up........you have to be held accountable for your actions.

Back in the 1970's I was the head coach at Plainfield High School in Plainfield, New Jersey. We had one of the top programs in the State. One day, three of my varsity players came (5 minutes) late to practice. At the end of practice they were disciplined (punished...some people may say)...during Opportunity Period for being late.

Opportunity Period (Immediately after practice), is time when a player may work with his position coach or with another player to get extra Reps on a skill he needed to improve. It was also a time when a player would get PUNISHMENT or discipline.

On this occasion, these 3 players were required to do bear crawls (all 4's) to make up for the fact that they were late. I GAVE THEM AN OPPORTUNITY TO CORRECT THEIR MISTAKE.. These ALL 4's are a real workout since we usually gave a minimum of 200 yards. We would bust their tail.

The next day....these same three players came late again. I approached them before practice and told them they had two choices;

1. hand in their equipment and leave the team....or

2. Take all of their equipment out of the varsity field house and move down to the 8th graders field house and practice with them for the next two weeks. If they were a problem of any sort, for the 8th grade coaches, they would be dismissed immediately from the team. They were shocked. They expected to do all 4's. One of the three was our starting right corner on defense. But....all 3 decided to clear out their locker and go to practice with the 8th graders. They knew that they could not play in any of the games and for two weeks they would have to be perfect at practice and needless to say....they had to be at practice on time.

After 2 weeks, the three players returned to the varsity. It took the starting corner two weeks to earn back his starting position. One of the other two players earned a starting spot in our defensive secondary for the last game of the season. He played a great game and earned the Defensive Back of the Week Award.

Opportunity Period was a time that we gave our players an *OPPORTUNITY* to get back in the good graces of the team.

BUT.......Discipline is a MUST.....
It is not what you do to someone.....
It is what you do FOR someone!

TRUST SYSTEM

This is an OUTSTANDING technique that I have learned during the years.

As a coach I was always interested in what the player thought was a good punishment .....a reasonable punishment.....a fair punishment. Remember what I previously said about APPEARING to be fair. This idea is very important in our Communication System.

If the player broke a team rule or did something that I thought deserved punishment of any sort (on the professional level we considered monetary fines).....before I decided on the type of punishment, I would ask the player;

- What do you think I should do?

I always wanted to see where the player's head was at.

I gave TRUST.

Many times the player would suggest a more harsh punishment than I would have given. This was interesting.

On some occasions I would give the player two or three choices. In this way, he would select his own punishment. In this technique, I would allow the player to administer HIS OWN punishment. I called this our TRUST SYSTEM.

We TRUST the player. Thus he can give himself his own punishment.

Always….and I mean always…..when the player did give himself his own punishment, the player would give 100% effort. He busted his tail. This was great. This system really worked.

I can truly say that the development of this TRUST SYSTEM in discipline was one of the greatest coaching achievements of my career. At least…this is what I believe.

Try it…..you will like it!

BEING HARD OR BEING RIGHT!

Through the years, on occasion, I would have a player or parent say to me, " Coach, you are being hard". My comment to that person was, "I never want to be hard…..I want to be right." As a coach I have no need in being a hard guy. I think if a coach wants to be a hard guy, he just may have a psychological problem.

I want to be right.

Remember when we were kids and our folks would say that you have to come home at a certain hour on Saturday night. Remember we always wanted to stay our later. Looking back, our parents were not trying to be hard. They really were trying to be right.

SOMETIMES…BEING RIGHT….APPEARS …….. THAT WE ARE BEING HARD.

Before, I discussed COMMUNICATION and that it was our most important system. When we discipline a player or punish (if you want to use that word) proper communication will help to sell the player on what we are doing and why! Remember….not only do we want to be fair……we always want to appear to be fair in regards to punishment and discipline.

PLAYER CONTRACT
- -

When I first started coaching in 1959 I had my first team meeting to explain all team rules and regulations. The next day we started practice, one of my players was late. He had to go to the dentist. I spoke with him about the need for him to be disciplined due to the fact that he was late and didn't give me a note from his parent about the dental appointment. He stated to me that he did not know he was supposed to bring a note ahead of time. I told him that this was discussed yesterday in our first team meeting about rules and he quickly told me that he wasn't at that meeting. Wow! He was right. I checked my attendance records and he was correct.

That winter, I went to a football clinic in Boston and I heard a coach speak about a PLAYER CONTRACT that he used with his team. What a great idea!

From that time on I always continued to use a player contract. The contract explained rules about attendance, lateness, academics, training rules, behavior towards parents, behavior in the community, etc. At the end of the contract, the player and his parent signed the contract........WITH MY HONOR! I or one of my coaches would also sign the contract. The parents received one copy and I kept a copy in the office. If a parent could not be in attendance for the meeting, an older brother or another relative could sub for the parent. If no one could come to the meeting, I or one of my assistants would go to the player's home to complete the contract signing.

The parents liked this contract idea. They would put it up on the refrigerator and remind their son when and if it was necessary to remind them of what was expected of him.

In 1975, one parent called me and said I have to CUT her son from the team. When I asked WHY?...she stated that she caught him smoking. Wow!

I always told the parents that they were an extension of the coaching staff once the player leaves our charge at school. This parent really took our suggestion to heart.

ORIENTATION MEETING – PARENTAL INTERFERENCE

I already mentioned our orientation meeting with the parents and players. But, as the years wore on it became more and more obvious that I would have to address words to our players parents about *parental interference.*

POSITIVE MIND SET

Through the years I developed a Positive Mind Set program for our players. The goal was to get the players *to make themselves better people.* If they could make themselves better people, then they could become better players. If they could make themselves better people, they would have a chance for a better future. To me.....this was and is more important than any football game we could win.

If they could become better players, we would have a chance to be a better team. And after all......one of the main goals is to WIN and you win with better players.

Remember......PLAYERS WIN!

In this Positive Mind Set Program, I adopted many of the Personal Developmental Skills and Concepts that I studied through the years. Concepts I took from coaches, business leaders, Statesmen, historians, and leaders in the field of Personal Development.

To try and minimize parental interference..... and this was usually about their son's PLAYING TIME. I tried to sell the parents on the need for their son to develop himself as an adult. I tried to sell the parent to help their son move from the child stage to the adult stage. I asked the parent to serve as their mentor. DON'T DO THE JOB FOR YOUR SON.......GIVE HIM INFORMATION....BE HIS

MENTOR....BE HIS ADVISOR AND LET HIM DO THE JOB..........LET HIM DO IT! In this way......he does it.....not the parent. The son grows as a human being.

I always used an example by telling the story of my father and what I learned from his life experience.

My dad was an immigrant from Greece. He was born in 1903 and only had a 3rd grade education. At the age of 12 he ran away from home and became a seaman. He traveled to all the countries bordering the Mediterranean Sea. Later at the age of 17, in 1920, his merchant ship traveled to America. He decided to jump ship in Norfolk, Virginia. He could not speak a word of English. He had no money. His parents were 7000 miles away. Who had to take care of business? He had to take care of business! There was no mommy or daddy to help. He was on his own. The umbilical cord was cut........ and he was only 17.....no money .....and he could not speak English.

He stopped a woman in the street and started talking to her in Greek. She guessed that he was talking in Greek and took him to a candy store that was owned by a Greek man. This was his lucky day. The candy store owner took him in and let him sleep upstairs above the store. He got his first job washing dishes and he learned how to make ice cream and candy.

The point I tried to stress to the parents was.....my Dad..... he had to get it done on his own. Parents of today have to allow their children to grow up and not always fight their battles for them.

I suggested to parents that if their son comes home and complains about not playing or if he complains about anything….. instead of the parent calling the coach or the teacher in school and fighting the son's battle…..the parent should give information to the son. Suggest how the son should approach the coach. Insist that he talk to the coach.

The next day, when the son comes home, ask the son how the meeting with the coach went. The parent needs to be an advisor…NOT the doer. In this way, the son DID IT….not the parent.

I always ask the parent…..which is better?….your son getting it done….or you as a parent doing it for your son? They know and always say it is better if their son DOES it.

This idea….this technique…..this sell to the parents has had great dividends. The parents stay out of the way and the player WILL MAKE himself better.

Remember, our goal is to get the player to MAKE HIMSELF A BETTER PERSON. A stronger person. A better person and stronger person can and will be a better player. A better player has a *better* chance to win.

"Hey Coach…….How Do You Win!"

DISCIPLINE!

SACRED COWS... PRIMADONNAS

A Star player can become a problem…a challenge. His head can become too big. He can become a negative distraction for the team and can cause morale problems which can lead to team failure....a LOSS! Remember ... *More Games are Lost Than Won!*

We stress to our teams that we will NOT HAVE ANY SACRED COWS. No one will get special treatment. Team morale is most important and players hate it when they see what they think is a coach's favorite...or one player is getting preferential treatment.

NO SACRED COWS...........NO PRIMADONNAS!

PRACTICE TIME

Practice time is when we PRACTICE. This may seem like a play on words but here is what I mean;

- Practice is the time when a player gets REPS on many different skills.

An example;

During practice our pass rushers work in a drill using many different techniques. Some techniques they will master. Other techniques they will not be very good at and need more REPS. We will REP in practice ....bull rush....speed rush......slap and swim....rip....etc.

Player A may have *mastered* only the speed rush and the rip. Player A must continue to REP the other techniques in practice in order to move to the next level of performance. Remember, this is his and his position coach's goal. Move to the next level of performance and increase productivity. Many players want to practice only the skills they do best. This is a mistake.

The player who only practices skills he does best will *never* have a chance to move to the next level of performance and increase his productivity. Lesser skills MUST get REPS....practiced.....until they are skills that have been MASTERED.

GAME TIME IS NOT PRACTICE TIME

On GAME DAY we want our players *not to practice*. We want them to use techniques they have *mastered*. This is GAME TIME....NOT PRACTICE.

Thus, on game day... Player A...... should concentrate on the two techniques that he has mastered. This concept will afford Player A the best chance to be successful in his pass rush attempts during the game.

Ed "Too Tall" Jones, the great defensive end of the Dallas Cowboys was a perfect example. He practiced many moves but when it came to game time, he stressed his speed rush technique because of all the moves he practiced, it was the speed rush that he did best. Many of his great plays were attributed to this specific technique.

The same concept is used in regards to *offensive plays*. We may practice a play in practice but never use the play in a game. *We will never use a play in a game unless we have MASTERED the play in practice.*

As a young coach I made this mistake and had to learn the hard way. I was fooled by using a play in a game that we only had two REPS in practice and the play worked for a TD. I was fooled into believing that I could continue practicing a play limited times in order for the play to be successful in a game. Failure of plays in games due to limited REPS made me learn......learn the hard way.

Practice time is for ...REPS....REPS....REPS and more REPS.

"Hey Coach......How Do You Win?"

Practice is practice.....and Game Time is Game Time!

POSITIVE REPS-NEGATIVE REPS

POSITIVE REPS......as compared to NEGATIVE REPS (waste of time). This concept is of major concern. A player will get POSITIVE REPS in practice when he goes 100% and when he does the REP correctly. Anything else is a NEGATIVE REP.

Sometimes in practice it appears that our players are going through the motions. They are developing negative reps. This will help us *lose* during game time. We have to coach the concept of MUSCLE MEMORY. The body and mind learn to do things without thinking. When we practice *negative reps......negative muscle memory* will develop bad habits and these BAD HABITS continue during game time.

The position coach MUST stress POSITIVE REPS in order to get MAXIMUM PRODUCTIVITY DURING PRACTICE.

This coaching technique is great coaching.

Eliminate NEGATIVE REPS.....otherwise practice is a waste of time.

OFFENSIVE CADENCE

In practice, Quarterbacks sometimes get into a rut by calling the snap number always on "one" or the "first sound". They do this over and over again without ever realizing what they are doing. The Coach has to make sure that this doesn't happen. If this happens in practice.........MUSCLE MEMORY kicks in and the offensive team, like zombies, anticipate and move on "one" or the "first sound". When the QB tries to change the snap count, the offensive line jumps off sides. I have seen this happen time and again, through the years.

I have been guilty of this poor coaching. Thus, at the very beginning of the season, the QB must be sold.....programmed on using multiple snap counts.

The defensive unit practicing against the offense can also be hampered by always going on "one " or the "first sound". They also need multiple counts practice to get used to the possibility in the game ...... So to not go off sides and give the opponent an easy five yards.

YOU PLAY LIKE YOU PRACTICE

" You play like you practice"....sometimes this is a hard sell to certain players. Certain players who are as NOT as coachable as they think they are, believe that they are *Gamers*. "Don't worry coach…..game time I will show you."

Unfortunately, there are some players who actually are *Gamers*. I try to sell this type player on the idea…*"can you imagine how good you could really be if you were a better practice player."*

Sometimes, this coaching suggestion works and sometimes it does not. But, this is why the coach has to be a *Master* teacher as Vince Lombardi said. The coach has to be a psychologist. The coach has to master people skills.

Remember, the coach's main responsibility is to get the player in his charge to move to the next level of performance.

This is one of the great challenges of coaching and it is what makes coaching so much fun.

LEARN HOW TO PRACTICE

Through the years, we have tried to sell our players that they must *learn how to practice.*

I stressed…"you have to learn how to walk to the locker-room……. you have to learn how to get dressed for practice………….you have to learn how to GET READY……you have to learn how to convince your teammates that you are into it!

This SKILL will create an atmosphere that will help us have a QUALITY PRACTICE.

Learning how to practice SHOULD be considered a SKILL. Just to get dressed and go out onto the practice field and go through the motions, is NOT practice.

- Quality practice leads to POSITIVE REPS

- Positive Reps leads to increased productivity.

- Increased productivity leads to better performance.

- Better performance leads to a better chance to win.

Remember......More games are lost than won.

Quality practice can help us to NOT lose.

"IF YOU CAN'T RUN, YOU CAN'T PLAY"

If you can't run, you can't play!   Oak trees don't move!

Football is a game of movement. In order to be great at this game you need to be able to move....and move quickly. Speed is necessary. But probably more important than speed is CONDITIONING. Vince Lombardi stressed............ "Fatigue makes cowards of us all". We try to sell our players on the concept, *"the Will to Win is not nearly as important as the will to prepare to win"*

This means work....work...and more work. Work is a NEGATIVE word to many people. Soooooo, we try to sell the idea that work is great. This is a MIND SET. And...... when we work there should be pain. Yes, we do use the saying...."no pain no gain" because it is the truth and players understand this idea.

In my book on POSITIVE MIND SET PROGRAM I stress concepts such as " average or special behavior"....and "take a negative and turn it into a positive". Selling these two concepts helps to teach our players to get more out of conditioning.

Conditioning has to occur during the pre-season....during the season and in the off season. As a coach you have to SELL the idea of conditioning 24-7. It never stops!

During practice, conditioning is best accomplished DURING practice and NOT after practice when drills such as wind sprints are usually done. By selling POSITIVE REPS the player actually is getting conditioning during practice.

PULSE RATE

In 1974 I read an article about the Interval Training System that was being used by the University of Tennessee swimming team. This system led me to recall how a great track coach by the name of Jim Fraley at Sewanhaka High School in Floral Park, Long Island, New York....used the pulse rate of prospective long distance runners to determine potential success. The average pulse rate for human beings is 70-72 beats per minute at rest. Coach Fraley was always looking for long distance runner candidates who had lower than normal pulse rates. If he found an athlete with a 60 or lower, he got real excited because he knew if this young person was coachable, he could develop into an outstanding long distance runner. Coach Fraley believed that this type athlete was working with a better circulatory and respiratory system and thus had more potential for long distance running than the average pulse rate athlete. He had to be right because Coach Fraley sent his guys all over the country on full scholarships as long distance runners. The walls of Sewanhaka High are full of plaques from the Penn Relays and almost all of them are for long distance runners.

The University of Tennessee used the pulse rate in their training of their swimmers. They tried to get their athletes to push themselves to be near 180 beats per minute. More than that and the average athlete would collapse. They tested their athletes during and after workouts. If an athlete had a pulse rate of lower than 140, the coach and the athlete knew that more effort was possible by the athlete.

For years I have used this pulse rate system to evaluate my players and their effort.

In 1976, while at Plainfield High in New Jersey, I had a young player by the name of Anthony Robinson. I tested him to have a 48 pulse rate at rest. After he ran a 12 minute run, I tested him again and his pulse rate was 52. WOW! This kid could run forever. In fact, after I ran him for 12 minutes without stopping…Tony said to me, "Coach…that was easy…..do you want me to do it again?" Tony played defense for me and while watching game film, it was a joy to watch him. During the fourth quarter of a game, it appeared that everyone but Tony was running in slow motion. Tony was flying all over the field making big plays. Thus, the moral of the story here is…use this system in FINDING players who have a God given ability to be in great physical condition. These players will make big plays for you in the second half when everyone else is tired. Remember, "you gotta win the 2nd half".

ENDURANCE CONDITIONING FOR THE LINEMEN

The running backs, receivers, D-backs all get plenty of running during practice. Linemen have close quarter drills and usually get work on quickness. BUT...BUT...linemen need work on ENDURANCE CONDITIONING.

Defensive linemen are usually selected for their quickness. Offensive linemen are usually selected for their size and ability to block. These BIG offensive linemen can and do get tired late in the ball game. It is during the 4th quarter when most sacks are given up by the offensive line. Tired legs allows the defense to get by the BIG offensive linemen.

Conditioning by the use of sprints for the offensive line, is not enough. They need ENDURANCE conditioning to build up the respiratory system so NOT to get tired. The huffing and puffing by the offensive line is what slows up their feet and legs. This is one area of coaching that I believe must be addressed and accomplished. NO EXCUSES. The big guys usually do not like this type of work. I had a lineman once say to me, "Coach, I am not a long distance runner." I said, "Yes you are!" You have to be able to GO THE DISTANCE at the same level of productivity.

This brings into play....the concept...."We must win the second half".

WE MUST WIN THE SECOND HALF

Conditioning…the ability to run at top speed for four quarters DETERMINES WHO WINS THE GAME. We always try to sell our team that "we must win the 2ⁿᵈ half".

Winning the 2ⁿᵈ half is one of our Team Goals when we play a game and we keep a chart on the bulletin board to show this accomplishment. There is a direct correlation between our team Won and Loss record and the Won and Loss record of the 2ⁿᵈ half.

Winning the second half shows us that we were in great shape….probably better than our opponents. Winning the second half also showed that *we didn't quit.* If we were losing at half time, winning the second half was a MUST.

Many times, I have had a player come up to me and say…"coach we have them on the run….they are tired!" Almost always…. this statement proved to be correct.

OVERLOAD PRINCIPLE

I first heard of this Overload Principle concept from Bud Wilkinson, the legendary coach at the University of Oklahoma in the late 1940's early 50's. The Overload Principle meant… .."make practice harder than the game will ever be. Thus…. the game will easy." This Principle stressed conditioning and the ability to overcome your opponent in the second half when he is more tired than you.

RACEHORSE FOOTBALL

Those Oklahoma teams of Wilkinson were known for *Racehorse Football.*

Racehorse Football was used during a time when players had to play both ways…..offense and defense. *Racehorse Football* was when the offensive unit went without a huddle. Much like what we do today in our Two Minute Offense…….with two exceptions.

1. *Racehorse Football* was done all game long, NOT just in the Two Minute situation.

2. In *Racehorse Football*, after every play the players would get off the ground quickly and sprint to their offensive alignment before the defense had a chance to get set. It was a revolutionary concept at the time and it drove opponents nuts. Needless to say, in order to play *Racehorse Football* you had to be in outstanding physical condition.

FINISH!

FINISH…..FINISH…FINISH…FINISH…every play. WOW!

This is a very important SKILL to teach. Yes, it is a SKILL OF THE MIND.

In evaluating game or practice tape, quite often we critique a player for becoming a FAN. On the snap, the player executed a move or block or he did whatever he was suppose to…. then he stopped….turned…and just looked at the play. He became what I call a FAN. If a player in practice can learn to NOT be a fan…..it will carry over into the actual game. His MOTOR will keep running.

We sell this concept by stressing to our players that if they become a FAN during practice or a game it must be because they are tired. They are not in good enough condition. Which means that they need to get more conditioning after practice in Opportunity Period. They need more work. They need more pain. We sell them that we as coaches have a responsibility to them to help them…coach them….to make sure they are in the best condition possible. If they are not FINISHING a play……they need help…….!

Right about now you are saying that I am being a wise guy. The player needs to self-discipline himself to FINISH each and every play…..during practice and this carries over into the game situation.

MUSCLE MEMORY AND MENTAL MEMORY

FINISHING will guarantee moving to the next level of performance and increased productivity.

When viewing tape with the team, we give great praise and recognition when players make a great FINISH on a specific play. We really make a big deal of it. Players like to hear their name mentioned in a positive way during these meetings……it is human nature.

Using game tape, we grade our players after every game. We stress that their grades can improve greatly when they FINISH a play. This grading system helps to motivate them to increase their ability to FINISH. Needless to say, the ability to FINISH will help us to have a better chance to WIN.

"Coach....how do you win?"

Teach them to FINISH baby!....FINISH!"

FINISH........ IT IS A MIND SET!

GAME TIME

- -

Game time! Show time! It is what we all practice for. Being in the arena. That is where the fun is. With our neck on the line. A time to compete. *IT IS WHAT WE LIVE FOR!*

During *Game Time* there are mental skills that coaches and players MUST learn in order to WIN. The following is a list of considerations that are needed to give our team a better chance at success.

RECOVER

- -

Vince Lombardi said…..RECOVER instantaneously…there will be many unsuccessful plays during a game. A player and or Coach…..must learn to NOT waste time on what has already happened. We have no control over "yesterday". Let us only think about "today and tomorrow".

In a football game, players will make mistakes. Players will drop passes....the QB will throw an interception....fumbles occur. We are aware of all the many possible mistakes that we can make.

Regardless, we must RECOVER instantaneously after each and every mistake. If a player hangs his head...and worries about the mistake he just made...he is not mentally prepared for the next play. It is at this time when real disaster usually happens.

An example;

-   A player dropped a pass. It was an easy pass that he should have caught. The player comes back to the huddle worrying about this pass that he should have caught. In the huddle he doesn't pay attention as he should have (he is thinking about the dropped pass) and he ends up lining up in the wrong formation causing the QB to have to call a time out. Consequence.....a wasted time out. A mental error. A BREAKDOWN.

In this situation, the player has to have *Thick Skin* and *Shake it off!* This is easier said than done.....BUT....it must happen if the player is to become a WINNER.!

In case you are wondering.....*Thick Skin* is the ability to not allow things to bother you. The opposite of *Thick Skin* is a *Thin Skin* person.

The ability to *Shake It Off* means the athlete must not allow the BREAKDOWN to take away his focus on the next play........*Shake it Off* and move on!

Bud Wilkinson, University of Oklahoma stressed in situations like this, teammates need to PUSH their teammates UP..... don't PUSH DOWN a teammate and make the situation worse. Wilkinson stressed ....this was a time for real leadership.....there is no time for feeling sorry for oneself........ can't waste time...or lose focus!

THE ENEMY IS THE CLOCK AND OURSELVES

Woody Hayes, Ohio State University said that THE ENEMY IS THE CLOCK AND OURSELVES. The minutes on the clock tick off and do not return during a game. Thus, the clock is something we have to conquer. TIME MANAGEMENT is an art and a coach needs many REPS to master this important phase of the game.

When a player wastes time feeling sorry for himself because of a mistake, he wastes the clock. Minutes and seconds we can not get back. Feeling sorry for our self is a sure way to LOSE.

"Hey Coach.....How do you Win?"

RECOVER............INSTANTANEOUSLY

Coach Hayes stressed that OURSELEVES is our opponent. Meaning that the first element we must conquer is OURSELVES. Our Mind Set. Our attitude. Our ability to RECOVER.

Remember, I mentioned before that we have no control over our opponents, the officials, the weather etc, BUT, we do have control over most things that we do. Our ability to CONTROL our mind set, our attitude, our ability to RECOVER will go a long way to overcoming the opponent called...OURSELVES.

More Games Are Lost Than Won!

INVEST IN PERCENTAGES

Being a student of the game meant to try and learn everything possible about this great game of football.

As a young coach I read everything I could get my hands on. As a student at Springfield College I would go to the college library and read any thesis that was about football. Several writings were concerned with percentages. This was my first learning of *playing the percentages.*

For example, on offense, if we had the ball on our own one yard line and had to go 99 yards for a TD, what was the likelihood....the percentages of this happening. The studies I read showed statistically that it was more than a 99-1 shot that the offensive team would go down and score a TD if they started with the ball in this example.

One of the main goals of the defense is to get the ball back for their offense in better field position than the offense had in their last possession. When the offense gets the ball in better field position, the percentages increase for the offense to score. Surveys showed that offensive drives over 12 plays usually breakdown unless the offense had a successful play of 30 yards or more.

In today's game, maybe the percentages are a little better due to a more sophisticated passing game. BUT....BUT....I am sure the percentages have not gotten better than 85-1 shot when the offense starts with the ball on their own 1 yard line. Still a small likelihood that the offensive team will score.

This information educates the offensive signal caller to consider what Bear Bryant suggested years ago. The ole Bear said..and I am paraphrasing, "struggle to get at least one first down....then use your punting game with great coverage to give you field position. Play great defense....attack the offense...strip the football.....help them create a mistake.... get a turnover. Better yet....struggle to get two first downs before you have to punt.

Now, with a great punt and great coverage, you have gained great field position." The Bear stressed that when in this type of a situation, you probably will not march down the field and score, BUT....BUT....proper strategy using the concept of INVESTING IN PERCENTAGES, will set up a score on your next possession. The PUNT is a TREMENDOUS OFFENSIVE WEAPON. The PUNT is not something by itself. When you consider the PUNT......the PUNT COVERAGE is equally important. This is one reason why the kicking game must be taught first and stressed to the highest level. Invest in percentages. Don't gamble...gamblers lose more often than not.....investors in percentages will win MORE over the long haul...

...the only time to gamble is when everything else fails and your up against a superior opponent....or the clock is against you.... when your choices are limited...gamble only after all percentage plays have failed.

A PLAN FOR EVERYTHING

Have a Plan for EVERYTHING! Bear Bryant sold this concept. I bought it, hook, line and sinker.

Have a plan for pre-game.......half time........and post game.

Have a Plan for halftime and we are;

> Winning and we are suppose to be winning
> Winning and we are suppose to be losing.......
> Losing   and we are suppose to be winning.......
> Losing   and we are suppose to be losing.........

Have a plan for your Post game talk and we;

> Won and we were suppose to win
> Won and we were suppose to lose
> Lost and we suppose to win
> Lost and we suppose to lose

Plan for every possibility that you can think of that might occur in a game.

This type of mental planning will give you great REPS in learning the game. Events that you think of, may never happen in a game, but have a PLAN..........*just in case!*

Plan for every minute of every week...in season and off-season.

GREAT ORGANIZATION can help you win.........POOR ORGANIZATION will most assuredly help you lose.

This concept will help your success ratio when you evaluate the.............10 Possession Rule.

ADJUSTMENTS

Have a PLAN for different adjustments that may have to be made during a game or during half-time. BE READY ahead of time. The old adage- "an ounce of prevention is worth a pound of cure", still holds up.

Your game plan is not worth the paper it's written on, if your GAME PLAN was made for only a situation where you are winning. Your GAME PLAN must be flexible so that adjustments can be easily made DURING THE GAME or DURING HALF-TIME if you are winning or losing.

Teach.....Two Ideas;

ANTICIPATION AND SUDDEN CHANGE!

Teach your players to *anticipate* the possibility of DISASTER....a BREAKDOWN........they will then *"be at the ready"* to RECOVER INSTANTANEOUSLY! They will have a PLAN to make whatever adjustments they need to make to continue their effort to win. No HEAD HANGING...No EXCUSES!   MOVE ON!....NEXT PLAY!......RECOVER!

Teach your players to anticipate the possibility of ....SUDDEN CHANGE.

BREAKDOWNS make us lose. Not being able to antici-pate and react quickly to sudden change is a very serious BREAKDOWN that we have CONTROL over. SUDDEN

CHANGE can be either a Positive or a Negative experience during a game.

A POSITIVE SUDDEN CHANGE

During a game we may recover an opponent's fumble.... or intercept an opponent's pass. BE READY for SUDDEN CHANGE. Don't fall asleep on the sidelines. Anticipate this SUDDEN CHANGE happening. EXPECT IT TO HAPPEN! ANTICIPATE SUDDEN CHANGE! And take advantage of the opportunity.

A NEGATIVE SUDDEN CHANGE

During a game, SUDDEN CHANGE can go against us. We could lose a fumble on offense and our defense has to be ready to fly back onto the field. No resting here! EXPECT THE POSSIBILITY! ANTICIPATE SUDDEN CHANGE!

Our MIND SET here, is to get the football right back. Steal the Football back. We must teach the mind set. .....STRIP THE BALL. *Create our own SUDDEN CHANGE!*

This type of a MIND SET must be taught.....it must be coached.

"Hey Coach......How do you Win?"

TEACH.... ANTICIPATION and SUDDEN CHANGE!

OFFICIALS

A MAJOR GOAL during game time is to try and take the officials out of the game. Try to eliminate the officials from being a factor.

Most officials are quality people and they try to do a great job. But, officials are human and on occasion it appears that an official has his own agenda during a game (for whatever reason). Maybe he had an argument with his wife that day. Who knows?

As a young coach I used to get all wound up during a game and I would really get on the officials. As the years went on, I LEARNED A BETTER WAY!

I learned that it was impossible for a coach to officiate and coach at the same time. I learned it was very difficult, if not impossible, to make objective decisions if I was in an emotional state.

I learned that I had to teach this concept....this MIND SET to my coaches and players...especially my coaches.

My coaches are SOLD on this concept and they are not allowed to talk to the officials during a game. We do not want an official,who has "rabbit ears" to be a factor in the game.

Previously, I talked about the 10 Possession Rule. One way to destroy one or more of our Possessions is to have penalties STOP us. Officials with rabbit ears can start throwing flags against us and thus destroy one or more game possessions.

This is a perfect example of.....WIN the officials. This is one of those factors WE HAVE CONTROL OVER!

"More Games Are Lost Than Won!"

KICKING GAME

- -

Through the years, I have heard many coaches say that the *Kicking Game* is the *Winning Edge.* I truly believe this. The *Kicking Game* is a tremendous PSYCHOLOGICAL weapon.

Through the years I have taken my own surveys concerning the *Kicking Game.*

In the Sunday newspapers, in the sports section…..during the football season….look up the scores of the college games that were played on Saturday. You can see games that were won by an extra point …or a field goal. In the write up about games you can read about the blocked kicks….the great punt returns…or the great kickoff returns or fumbles committed during the *Kicking Game.* I estimated that one/third of all games were won or lost due to the *Kicking Game.* Stressing the *Kicking Game* IS the *Winning Edge.*

PRE-SEASON

In the Pre-Season, much emphasis is placed on FINDING key personnel for the *Kicking Game.*

We screen daily for long snappers....punters...punt receivers....place kickers....kick return men. We sell our players on the *Kicking Game.*

In 1980, while I was head coach at St. Thomas Aquinas High School in North Edison, New Jersey, we found, through our screening, a young man named Joe Nisky who had a great knack for getting"skinny" on kick block attempts. During that season Joe went onto blocks several punts and extra point attempts. He was not FAST on the stop watch but he sure played QUICK during game time.

DURING THE SEASON

We use our BEST players in the *Kicking Game.* We stress that the *Kicking Game* is not a time for REST. We give great recognition in the *Kicking Game.*

For Every game we recognize a SPECIALTY TEAM PLAYER OF THE WEEK. We use Stars decals for our helmets as part of our Recognition System. A Star System that I started to use back in 1961. I was coaching on Long Island and I had to buy my stars from a company in California. Coach Goldstein in Central Islip was the only other coach in the area using Stars so there was no need for local venders to carry Stars decals. As the years went by, other symbols came into vogue such as Skull and Cross Bones, Footballs, Warriors, etc.. It was then that local vendors started to carry helmet decals and other schools started to use these motivational recognition symbols.

We give out a great number of Stars for achievement in the *Kicking Game*. Our players look forward to having great FUN by being a part of the *Kicking Game* teams.

After a game, when I talk to the newspaper reporters, I always try to mention KEY plays that occurred during the *Kicking Game*. I try to get the reporters to write about these great plays.

Football is a MIND GAME. When your opponent scores a TD and kicks off to you, only to have you return the kickoff for a TD, it nullifies the TD they just scored. This is a great PSYCHOLOGICAL weapon.

PRE PRACTICE

Most teams practice the *Kicking Game* in Pre-Practice....as we do too. In Pre-practice we are always trying to FIND new players to fit into our *Kicking Game* depth charts.

DURING PRACTICE

We start off every practice session by doing one or two phases of the *Kicking Game*. We practice the Kicking Game FIRST, before we do offensive or defensive segments of practice.

Thus we SELL the importance of the Kicking Game by stressing to the team that it is so important that we practice the Kicking Game FIRST.

POST PRACTICE - OPPORTUNITY PERIOD

After practice we use a session we call.....*Opportunity Period.* During this session we do different INDIVIDUAL skills..... REPS. Besides REPS in offense or defense skills we get extra REPS in the individual skills of the *Kicking Game*......such as practice of onside kicks....pooch punts and kickoffs...long snaps...holds...fake extra point or field goal attempts, etc.

SCORING IN THE KICKING GAME

We put tremendous emphasis on SCORING in the Kicking Game. Any time our opponent kicks the ball to us..WE GET EXCITED! WOW!

This is a great chance to BLOCK a kick. This is a great chance to SCORE and create....THIS WINNING EDGE! A long kick return is a great PSYCHOILOGICAL WEAPON.

If we don't score on a kick return, our goal is to get a great return. Once again, we give GREAT recognition to all team members when we make great plays in any phase of the *Kicking Game.*

The Kicking Game IS the Winning Edge!

PAT OR 2 POINT CONVERSION

We have had tremendous success with the MUDDLE HUDDLE during a extra point attempt.

The whole team, except for the snapper, the holder and kicker.....line up on the left hash mark (3 yard line). We use different calls by the holder. The call will either tell the team to line up for the placement kick or the call will tell the team which of 2 or 3 possible 2 point conversion attempts we will try. The call is always based on the defensive alignment and readiness of our opponent.

This strategy insures that our opponent better be prepared, otherwise they will get burned with a successful 2 point conversion against them. The MUDDLE HUDDLE is another facet of the game that our opponents must prepare for. This is another great psychological weapon..

"Hey Coach.......How Do You Win?"

The Kicking Game IS.....IS.....IS...the Winning Edge!

BILL MCKENNA TO STU SHOLL.....
THE KICK BY PAUL NELSON

The year is 1966. First game of the season vs. Mepham High School at our place. We are the Sewanhaka Football Indians of Sewanhaka HS from Floral Park, Long Island, New York. It is raining like mad. A torrential downpour. The score is 6-6. There are 6 seconds left in the game. We have the football. I call a time out. I throw out the kicking tee for an attempt at a 37 yard field goal. Rain or no rain our big center, Bill McKenna snaps the ball to our holder, Stu Scholl.

Paul Nelson, our QB is our placekicker. Scholl places the ball. Nelson goes through with the kick. The line blocks. The ball is up. It is going…going….it skins the right upright and goes in for a successful field goal. We win with no time on the clock….9-6. The place goes crazy. This was the first field goal the school kicked in 20 years. Everyone is rolling around in the mud.

"Hey Coach…….How do you win?

The Kicking Game Baby……the Kicking Game.

OFFENSE...
CONCEPTS AND...
OBSERVATIONS OVER THE YEARS...

In Chapter 2 ....I mentioned the 10 Possession Rule and many factors that went into evaluating POSSESSIONS. In this Chapter, stressing offense, please refer back to Chapter 2 and important concepts such as;

- 3 Categories of Plays....Direct, Delayed and Special

- Run Game....where do you attack?

- Pass Game..........Test them!

- Gamble or Invest

- The Off Tackle Hole

- Down and Distance

- Hash Mark

- Quick Hitters

- A Plan for everything

- Multiple Offense

Add to Chapter 2 the following important offensive considerations that I have learned through the years.

MULTIPLE OFFENSE PACKAGE

In Chapter 2 and Chapter 5, I tried to SELL you on the importance of a MULTIPLE OFFENSE.

Multiple....means Multiple. Meaning that you NEED in your Offensive package, plays that give your team the ability to take advantage of every weakness of a specific defense.

If defensive tackles playing over the interior are taught to "go up field.....go up field" (such as in the 43 defense)..... you have to have trap plays in your offense to take advantage of this weakness. It is easier said than done for the defensive coordinator to tell his tackles to close down to stop the trap, but it is harder for the defensive tackles to do this because it takes practice...REPS to develop trap reaction. Especially since the DT's have been spending a lot of time practicing "get up field" to get great pressure on the passer.

Multiple Means Multiple and a Multiple Offensive Package should include;

- *The Sneak...*

   The #1 play in your offense.....forces the defense to cover the A gaps.

- *dives*...quick hitters....only screen blocks needed...tough to defend

- *traps*....take advantage of up field linemen.....angle block ....possible double team at point of attack.

- *counters*....take advantage of LB's flying to football..... freeze middle linebacker in 43 defense...

- *sweeps*......must stretch defense horizontally to create ability to run vertically with (dives and powers)

- *tosses*... same concept as sweeps but quicker

- *powers*...both inside A and B gaps as well as outside in C and D gaps.

- *off tackles*......must be able to take advantage of the MOST vulnerable hole on the defensive front.

- different type *Options* in the option game......speed option...... counter speed option, trap option, double and triple option

- different *passes* (play action...sprintouts.... Bootlegs.... 3-5-7 step ....dropbacks).....screens and draws...!

These plays are needed in the MULTIPLE OFFENSIVE PACKAGE. Specific plays can be stressed during the week taking into consideration the defensive scheme of your upcoming opponent.

SURVEY

Several years ago I started to take my own survey of *success and failure* of the *running game*. On Sunday and Monday mornings, I would look at the daily newspapers and read game statistics of college and pro games. I learned that 90 % of the teams that won…had more rushing yards than their opponent.

Very few winning teams WON having less rush yards than their opponents. The WINNERS put more into their RUN game. They INVESTED MORE into their run game.

The average fan may not be aware of this statistic. Many fans think that the passing game is the most important factor in winning.

You have to be able to RUN the football. The ability to RUN the football sets up the passing game. It can be said that the passing game sets up the run game. Yes, sometimes…..but it is not the same. If a team can not run the football success-fully, the defense can sit back and play better pass defense.

This is a proven fact when you consider two great quarter-backs (Bret Farve- Green Bay Packers and Dan Marino-Miami Dolphins) who had great careers passing the football but when they had difficulty winning in their careers it was due to an inadequate running game.

Remember, the *Run Game* can control the clock and shorten the game. The *Run Game* can help your defense if they are *not great*….. by keeping them off the field.

THE ART OF PLAY CALLING

Some coaches say that the *Art of play calling* is a lost Art. Offensive play callers are criticized for using a GRAB BAG offense or so it seems. A GRAB BAG offense is the type of offense when it appears that the play called has no real rhyme or reason for it's selection. The coach simply puts his hand in a bag and pulls out a play. I am being sarcastic but it sure seems that there is a big question on why many plays are called.

TV analyst, John Madden has said time and again, (I am paraphrasing)...."I don't see a reason for that play call!". Even ole John agrees.

When evaluating the 10 Possession Rule.....it is offensive play calling where the most mistakes occur. If the coach gets better in this area, his win percentage is guaranteed to get better.

His team will NOT LOSE. Remember, *More Games are Lost Than Won!*

The Art of Play Calling comes into play with the game plan that will be in use. The game plan in use has to take into consideration WHAT the team has available in their *offensive arsenal*. Only by being MULTIPLE will a team have an arsenal that *can do it all!*

Some coaches believe that to *do it all* is too much. They feel that their team can not learn that much and thus will *Breakdown*. And....we know what BREAKDOWNS will do! I agree and disagree. I believe that the fun in coaching is to *teach*. I believe that players can learn. I believe that great coaching insists on high *expectations*. I have coached at all types of schools. Rich schools where the students were suppose to be smart and I found out we had our share of "not so smart" kids. I coached at all minority schools where the students were so called….disadvantaged….and the academic expectations was they would be academically slower. NONSENSE. Challenge your players. They CAN learn. Build self confidence and you will see how much they can learn. I DO believe that if your players CAN NOT LEARN to *Do it all* then your team WILL BREAKDOWN and stop themselves because they are limited to what they can do.. Thus, the coach has to be a *Student of the Game* and become a great teacher. Remember what Lombardi said, "we don't coach football, we coach people." Remember ole Jake Gaither who said, "football is not about X's and O's….. football is about Billy's and Joe's."

TEACH…TEACH.

I am also reminded of what Coach Ozzie Solem said to me way back in my college playing days, "Remember….it is not how much you know that counts…..it is how much your players know that counts."

Soooooo….a coach has a dilemma. Be 100 % prepared….or NOT 100% prepared.

In order to be 100% prepared, the offensive package must includes plays from all categories. The coach has to be a great teacher. Test his players. Make sure they know what they are doing. Then get his players mentally and physically prepared to get it done.

Easy? ……yea ….sure……right!   No…not easy….but it sure is great fun and great coaching!

Let me give you some information. I may not be politically correct in saying this but I hate all that stuff about being politically correct.....especially when I think some folks are wrong.

I was born and raised in New York City, on 135th Street in a section called Harlem. I was a white kid living in a black environment (colored was the word in those days). I went to school with black kids and I knew there were plenty who were smart. Smarter than I was. I also heard Jake Gaither, the legendary coach from Florida A&M talk in 1961 before the Civil Rights movement really got kicked off. Ole Jake tried to sell coaches from around the country to have the same expectations of colored kids as they do white kids, Sooooooo......when I got to be a head coach at an all black school, I insisted on HIGH EXPECTATIONS. *I did not say,* "Oh.....my poor black kids can't learn all this stuff." Instead, I said "Yes.....they can learn." AND WE WENT OUT AND PROVED IT WITH GREAT TEAMS learning all that I am mentioning in this book.

I had players whom the school said could not read. Well, on the football field they were able to read defenses.

Teach.....and any player can learn! Teach!

19 FACTORS TO CONSIDER IN THE ART OF PLAY CALLING

Some of these factors were discussed in Chapter 2. Others need to be discussed.

1. DECISION... DO WE RUN OR PASS?

- - *If we decide to run the football......*do we go direct or delayed or special?

- - We will GO DIRECT if we believe we are better at the point of attack than our opponent.

- - We will GO DELAYED if our opponent is better.

- - We will use a SPECIAL play only if everything else has failed or on some occasions if we are in a FREE down situation.

If we decide to pass. We have learned that the best down to pass the football, in all surveys taken, is FIRST DOWN when the defense is anticipating the great possibility of a running play. To take advantage of the defensive anticipation of a run play, the pass should be a PLAY ACTION PASS. To show dropback or shot gun, makes it easier for the defense, even though you can run the football from dropback move-ment or a shotgun formation.

When we pass the football, we must have a GOAL. Do we pass for a first down? Do we pass trying for a long gainer? Do we pass trying for a TD?

If we are passing for a first down, we must call passes that will get the yardage needed. Sounds like common sense..... doesn't it? So often we see BREAKDOWNS by the offense when they run patterns that will not get first down yardage. Maybe the coach calling the play thinks the receiver will catch the ball and run for the first down yards.

Yea…..maybe! A gamble. Or do you INVEST in a pattern that has the needed yards for the first down if the ball is caught and the receiver gets tackled immediately? I guess you know the answer!

If we are going to pass……..do we SHOW pass right now, or do we use PLAY ACTION. If the whole world knows we need to pass the football, then we are going to SHOW pass right now. If we do not have to pass the football, we can run or fake a run, which can even be better and use PLAY ACTION. Remember the advantages of the PLAY ACTION PASS…..attack the defenders that have two responsibilities…. run and pass. They can't do both.

FIELD ZONES

RUN or PASS will depend on many factors. Time left in the half or the game. The weather. The score. But usually, the most important factors are DOWN AND DISTANCE and FIELD ZONE.

Play selection should be influenced by FIELD ZONES.

THE COMING OUT ZONE

The Coming out zone….from the offensive team's own goal line to their own 35 yard line.

- This zone is normally considered a 3 down zone. The offense needs 3 1/3 yards per play for a first down, otherwise they have to punt on 4th down.

- mistakes here will kill you.

- offensive plays MUST BE SAFE PLAYS. Multiple ball handling can be disastrous. Usually the Goal here is to get one or two first downs and then if you must punt, you will have better field position.

Throwing passes laterally such as in a wide receiver screen are low percentage plays (as far as getting a first down is concerned). When they work, they look great BUT.......

Four things can happen.

1. Incomplete pass.

2. Complete pass for limited or no gain.

3. Great chance for lineman deflection and possible INT

4. Complete pass for good yardage.

Only 1 in 4 chances of GOOD things happening.

- Get UP FIELD with your passing game...don't WASTE a down. Curls......flood patterns......crossing patterns.

- Passes with STOPPING patterns are good...... Curls...... hooks.....comeback patterns to the outside.

- Passes with BIG WINDOWS ARE BEST. Passes with a lot of room, with the field, are BIG WINDOW Patterns. The Post.......Post Corner routes...usually are BIG WINDOW patterns......2 deep cover gives opportunity for 4 deep patterns (4 verticals) which can result in a BIG WINDOW. Passes thrown to the sideline more often than not are patterns with SMALL WINDOWS. Corner routes, out patterns, usually are SMALL WINDOW patterns.

- Run and pass at the weakness of a specific defense.

- Run game or pass game must have the ability to AUDIBLE to a better play if the defense is stacked to stop or make difficult the offensive play first selected.

- The Goal here is to get into the Freedom Zone so the offense can use their entire offensive package.

THE FREEDOM ZONE

The Freedom Zone....from the 35 to the 35 yard line.

- Free to use entire offensive package

- Most difficult zone for the defense to DEFEND because offense can do ANYTHING.

- Offense is FREE to call any type play.

- This is a 3 down zone until the offense crosses the 50 yard line.

- Great zone on the field for use of a FREE down play selection such as a fade pattern off play action.

- Goal is to get into the scoring zone.

THE SCORING ZONE

- Some coaches say the Scoring Zone or Red Zone is from the Opponents 20 yard line and in!

- Others have a zone for the 5 yard line on in! We call this zone.... the Black Zone!

- Defense usually starts gambling here because their back is to the wall. Play action pass has high percentage of success because run support defenders have to respect run fake......then react to pass coverage.

  Crossing patterns with your tight ends can be very effective.

- Only 2 ½ yards needed per play....thus a great RUN game is a MUST in this zone. As mentioned above, it will force the defense to attack and respond to run play setting up the play action pass.

Regardless.....where ever and how ever you break up the field for zones, the Game Plan will have *Play Selection* listed in each of these zones.

These plays MUST take into consideration whether the zone is a 2 or 3 or 4 down zone.

2. DOWN AND DISTANCE

Plays need to be selected based on the FIELD ZONE and *Down and Distance.*

Down and Distance in each of the different FIELD ZONES means different plays should be used based on the number of yards needed for a first down......*"Move the Chains"*

Plays should be charted for;

- 1st and 10.................1st and 5..........1st and long

- 2nd and short............2nd and medium........2nd and long

- 3rd and short............3rd and medium.......3rd and long

- 4th and short............4th and medium........4th and long

Short yardage can be anywhere from 1-3 yards. Medium yardage can be anywhere from 3-6 or 7 yards. Long yardage can be anywhere from 7 plus yards.

Another concern is the FIELD ZONE the offense is in and the time remaining in the first half or the game.

3. OLD RELIABLE PLAYS

I suggest very strongly that it is sound football for the offensive coordinator to have a list of plays that he can classify as *Old Reliable Plays*. Plays that have been good to him through the years, or plays that have been successful during the present season. A coach needs these *Old Reliable Plays* to go to as a part of his game plan BUT more importantly he needs to make sure that these plays are used....and used.....and used. Especially in critical situations.

As a young coach I learned this concept from Buddy Parker who was the head coach of the Detroit Lions in the 1950's. He called these *Old Reliable Plays*, his *Bread and Butter Plays*.

4. 2 DOWN ZONE

On occasion a team may find themselves faced with a possible *2 Down Zone.* This happened to us years ago during a game we played in a torrential rain storm. I had learned that in conditions like these, it may be better to allow your opponent to have the football on offense and try to force an error....a fumble....deep in their own territory. Thus, the punt became the most important offensive weapon we had that day.

We punted on 3rd down on several occasions. We ended up winning the game but after the game, the reporters we quick to question why I was punting on 3rd down so often. Several of our fans were also wondering. I explained to the Press that if we punted on fourth down, deep in our territory, our opponent would probably put on a maximum punt block attempt. They had to know that deep in our own territory, with the weather as bad as it was, we would not gamble on 4th down. In this situation, with the mud and rain, the chance of a blocked punt increased.

By punting on 3rd down, our opponent was not sure that we were going to punt. We may use a punt fake.(We had a Fake Punt Series but didn't use it). It also gave us an extra down to punt the football in case we had a bad snap or a fumbled snap by the punter due to the weather. I learned this strategy by reading football books written by the great coaches of America. By following the suggestion of my ole college coach, Ozzie Solem, who said....*Be A Student Of The Game!*

5. 3 DOWN ZONE OR 4 DOWN ZONE-

A coach has to make a decision to whether or not his offense is in the 3 down or 4 down zone. This has a great bearing on play selection. The fact that your team is in the 3 down or 4 down zone along with Down and Distance has great bearing on whether or not you attempt a *Running Play* or a *Pass Play*.

If the offense is in the 3 down zone, they need *3 1/3 yards per play*. If they do not MOVE THE CHAINS for a first down, on 4th down they have to punt.

If the offense is in the 4 down zone, they only need *2 ½ yards per play* to move the chains. On 4th down, while in the 4 down zone, it is not necessary to punt the football.

Play selection is quite a bit different for the coach who uses these considerations in his play selection.

Some coaches LOVE the field goal and when they are in the 4 down zone. Their play selection leans towards a 3 down zone philosophy. On 4th down, they are going to attempt to kick a field goal regardless. This thinking changes your Down and Distance NEEDS.

Other coaches think 4 down zone all the way when in the 4 down zone. On 4th and short.....they will go for the first down or a TD and forsake the field goal attempt (except late in the half or at the end of the game when strategy dictates a field goal attempt.). This type of thinking permits the coach calling offense to believe that he only needs 2 ½ yards per play and this fact gives him more room for error since he needs less yards per play.

The coach who develops a great running game is very hard to stop in the 4 down zone. I much rather face a passing team when my opponent is in the 4 down zone. Through the years, statistics prove this point to be correct.

I heard Lee Corso talk when he was coaching at the University of Indiana. He stressed a coaching concept that I still believe today. On 4th and short....say 4th and 1 .... Corso said that in the first half.....go for the first down or the TD. Corso said that in the second half, go for the points....the field goal. The logic here, is that in the second half, you may not get down that close to the goal line again....get the points. I believe this to be a *sound* offensive strategy. (Naturally, the score could change this philosophy).

When we forced our opponent to attempt a field goal while they were in the Red Zone or near the goal line, I considered this a STOP and a defensive win accomplishment for us. In fact, I would be glad to give my opponent 4 field goals on 4 possessions for a total of 12 points. We only need to score twice and get one extra point in 4 possessions to be leading in the game 13-12.

We try to sell our team that when we are in the 4 down zone, we SHOULD GET A TD ON EVERY OCCASION. If do not accomplish this goal.....we FAILED....we BROKEDOWN. We STOPPED OURSELVES. If we do not get a TD, we either made physical or mental mistakes to stop ourselves OR......I as the coach called the WRONG PLAYS. I truly believe that wrong play selection happens over and over again. Wrong PLAY SELECTION based on CONCEPTS

I am writing about in this book, has stopped more offenses than the defense ever has. It goes back to what Bear Bryant said, "More Games Are Lost Than Won!"

6. THE SCORE AFFECTS PLAY SELECTION

We start off every game with a MIND SET that we are losing 6-0. We never think that the score is 0-0. Our goal is to create a keen "sense of urgency." Our goal is to play like we are behind. Our attitude is that we have to score first and kick the extra point to go up 7-6.

If we score first, our MIND SET changes and now there is NO SCORE…it is 0-0!

When we are ahead in a game, we always try to play the game as if we are losing. We try to trick our mind to not become complacent and relax on a lead.

God forbid we are losing. Our MIND SET in this situation becomes exaggerated. If we are losing 7-0…..we say…. "we're losing 14-0". We make it worse than it is. WE TRY TO CREATE THAT SENSE OF URGENCY…that is needed to RECOVER…AND WIN!

The score affects play selection and tempo.

7. TEMPO

The *Tempo* of the game is controlled by the SCORE and TIME remaining. This MUST be practiced in offensive team period. Many a game has been lost due to inadequate *TEMPO* control by the offense. Wrong T*EMPO* is a BREAKDOWN that we have *CONTROL* over.

"More Games Are Lost Than Won! "

8. TIME

Time left in the first half or time left in the game...dictates type of plays to be used. *Time Management* MUST be practiced in Offensive Team period.

Bill Walsh, San Francisco 49'ers...stressed.....Practice time must be given to;

- 4 plays left in the half or the game.

- 3 plays, 2 plays and one play left in the half or the game.

These critical situations must be practiced to eliminate Coaching BREAKDOWNS.

So often players are blamed for mistakes made in these critical situations but the truth is that the players probably did not have enough REPS in practice to be able to execute these plays successfully. Thus, we have COACHING BREAKDOWNS ......NOT PLAYER BREAKDOWNS.

9. WEATHER

Many people think that if it rains, it hurts the team that wants to pass the football. Just the opposite CAN be TRUE. The defensive back is going backwards. The offensive receiver is going forward. Who has the advantage in the MUD? If the QB can get the ball in the air to the receiver, great things can happen in the passing game on a rainy day.

10. INJURIES

Injuries can destroy a Game Plan as far as play selection is concerned. Thus, the well prepared coach has PLANNED for this possibility. Remember what Coach Bryant said...... "Have a Plan for Everything".

You have to have a comprehensive substitute list "at the ready" for all injury possibilities. You also have to have a list of plays that can be used when these subs are in the game. If you call plays where the subs did not have enough reps to be successful, you as the coach put your player in a position to fail. This goes back to the statement I previously made.... The Coach's responsibility is to put his players in the best position to be successful.

11. PLAYS THAT ARE DOING WELL

I use a coach in the Booth to record our offensive plays. Success and Failure charts are necessary. The Coach in the Booth is responsible for reminding our signal caller to NOT forget plays that were successful. So often we see a team run a successful play and never use that play again in the same game.

If it works.....run it to death!

Eleven straight times!-

Back in the 1960's I was coaching at Sewanhaka High School in Floral Park, Long Island, New York. We had a big game vs. Berner High who was riding a 33 game winning streak. It was a tough hard fought physical battle....a low scoring game. We were losing 7-0 in the 4th period. We got the ball with 10 minutes left in the game. I decided to try and ram the ball down the throat of the Berner High defense.

My decision was......let's go right at them. No fooling around. We started our drive on our own 20 yard line. On the first play, we went off right tackle with our Fullback Guy Tripodi running behind the blocking of Bob Annunziata. We gained 4 yards. On second down....we ran the same play. A play we called our 35 Power. On the 3rd down we ran the same play. On 4th down we ran the same play. We ran the same play eleven straight times. Same ball carrier over the same lineman. Same point of attack.

We scored to make the score 7-6 Berner. With no over- time rule, the decision was to go for a 2 point conversion. We tried a pass for the two-point conversion …..we failed on the attempt and lost the game. The point here is …….if it works….use it!   Force them to stop it! Berner could not stop the play for 11 straight attempts.

12. SUB IN THE GAME ETC.

A substitute for us will affect if we run a specific play. Did the sub get enough REPS in practice so we can successfully run the play. This was stated before previously, but worth mentioning again….MENTAL REPS! This concept is very important to remember if we do not want to BREAKKDOWN our Possession. This judgment must be made….and made quickly during a game.

A substitute for the defense of our opponent will give us information as to a possible weakness in their defensive unit. A play selection decision here, may tell us to attack this SUB immediately. If we do not take advantage of our opponents SUBSTITUTION than this could end up being a MENTAL breakdown by the coaching staff.

More Games Are Lost Than Won!

SPECIAL NOTE HERE!

13. EYES... EYES... EYES OF THE DEFENSE

I think that sometimes offensive coordinators forget that the real weakness of the defense is their EYES. The EYES of the defense tell them what to do. Thus there are times we must fool their EYES. Defensive backs take their eyes off their receivers. Linebackers read the flow of the ball or the QB after they read the keys of offensive linemen with their EYES. Defensive linemen will LOOK with their EYES after they react after the snap of the ball.

EVERYONE ON THE DEFENSE WANTS TO LOOK FOR THE BALL.

I have already stressed the importance of going DIRECT. The importance of challenging the defender. Find out if you can beat him. In the passing game remember that Al Davis liked to test them deep and test them early. Vince Lombardi liked to attack the defense DIRECT early and at the defense's strength....to test them. Lombardi believed if you beat their best defender, you broke their defensive chain at it's strongest link.

BUT......BUT.....if you are playing against great people you will need to take advantage of their EYES and use a delayed play....misdirection. Get the defense moving one way and counter back away from their movement. This requires great ball handling (faking) by the QB. Some people say that "Faking" by QBs is a LOST ART. The QB's ability to hide the ball or hide his hands after a handoff is a skill that must be STRESSED and developed.

How many times do we see defensive backs sneaking a look into the offensive backfield, only to get beat deep by a receiver. I wish I had a dollar for every time this occurs. This is where the play action pass comes into play. Especially on a run down situation.

When an offensive lineman shows pass protection immediately, the defensive lineman pins his ears back and attacks with his pass rush techniques. On play action, the offensive lineman *should be attacking the defender with a run block technique and then go into pass protection.* This is very helpful to the QB and the offensive lineman. The defender's EYES reads run first, then pass....thus he should be late in trying to get to the QB. Again....another reason for play action pass on run down.....first down.

There was a time in the dropback passing game when offensive lineman were taught AGGRESSIVE and PASSIVE pass blocking techniques. AGGRESSIVE pass blocking taught the lineman to ATTACK first then recoil into a PASS SET mode. The PASSIVE technique is what is usually taught today with the offensive lineman using a PASS SET position immediately upon the snap of the ball. Years go offensive linemen were encouraged to mix it up and keep the defender off balance by using either AGGRESSIVE or PASSIVE techniques.

How many times have you seen teams use a dropback pass on first down? Over and over and over again. This is *Bad Play Selection.* The offense is making it easier for the defenders who have run support and pass coverage responsibilities.

Only in certain situations is a dropback pass called for on first down and this is usually because of limited time left in the half or the game.

Play action passes force the linebackers to BITE onto the running fake. Receivers now have more space to get open in the defensive second level and the soft under belly of the third level of defense especially if the defense is in zone cover.

When a huge chunk of yards are needed, many coaches feel that a pass is necessary. Many times when a pass is completed, it looks SO EASY. BUT….BUT….if the coach builds a great ground game, a running play can end up gaining as much yards as a pass play.

I am not saying that the coach should forgo the pass for a running play. I am saying that the coach has to have both possibilities. No excuses.

I have heard coaches say that they don't have many players that can catch the football. Nonsense. Train them. REPS… REPS….and more REPS.

In the off-season, get a basketball and have your potential receivers do ball drills off the side of the school building. Doing both one hand and two hand drills. These drills are great for developing great eye hand coordination. The receiver should do at least 1000 REPS off the wall each day in the off-season. You will find out you can develop players with great hands. You will find out who WANTS TO PAY THE PRICE FOR SUCCESS.

I have heard coaches say that they do not have a running back worth a dam. Nonsense. Somewhere on your team you have more than one player who can become a fine running back.

FIND HIM! Screen your players.

On the high school level, many coaches put their big guys on the line and end up with a PONY backfield of small guys. Why not take one of your big linemen and develop a BIG fullback or Tailback? I always did this. I always want to have a BRAMA BULL in my backfield. They are tough to tackle.

Tough to bring down. Remember when Mike Ditka used the Refrigerator on the goal line when he coached the Chicago Bears?

14. USING THE FIELD

Taking advantage of the hash marks....the wide side of the field will add information to the FIELD zone and the DOWN zone information in play selection. Running into the boundary can be tough. Remember ole Sammy Sideline.... the boundary.....he never missed a tackle in his career.

If you run to the wide side of the field....trying to get horizontal stretch....then your great back can read the defense and do his thing.....cut up or continue outside. He can FIND the running lane.

You might say, "Well....if you always run to the wide side... they will slant in that direction." SO WHAT! Use angle blocking, not direct blocking. Woody Hayes said.......THEY STILL HAVE TO STOP YOU.

If your opponent continues to always slant to the field, you have them set up for a direct play up the middle or a misdirection play to the boundary. The *mistake* is to run a DIRECT play to the boundary. REMEMBER what was just covered about the EYES of the defense. The defense will LOOK at the DIRECT play and have an easier time defending such a play. They will fly to the ball. On DIRECT plays to the boundary, Sammy Sideline becomes their extra player. By using a Misdirection Play, a Delayed Play to the boundary, the offense is taking advantage of the EYES of the defense by getting defenders to react a specific way.....to the field on the first fake. The odds of a Misdirection Play NOW working have increased.

15. USING HORIZONTAL AND VERTICAL STRETCH

This is also an important consideration in the game plan.

Do we throw deep first, *to test them* and *to set up the short passing game....* or do we *establish the short passing game to set up deep passes?*

In the run game......do we go wide to get horizontal stretch *to set up the inside direct running game?......*or do we pound inside *to set up sweeps and tosses....the outside game?*

We MUST take horizontal and vertical stretch into consideration in play selection in developing our game plan AND in making game time adjustments. Proper consideration here will help us to NOT...BREAKDOWN....or NOT destroy a possession. NOT create Coaching error.....NOT WASTE a possession.

But remember....our game plan may change...we must be ready to make adjustments...ANTICIPATE.....SUDDEN CHANGE. This is where the experience of the coach comes into play...... REPS BABY.....COACHING REPS!

16. MOST VULNERABLE HOLE

Don't forget *THAT* off tackle hole that was discussed earlier in this book.

17. WHAT IS BAD PLAY SELECTION?

If you are a wise guy, you will say that the only *Bad Play Selection* is a play called that did not work. Ha Ha...... " Hey....wise guy!"

Play selection should be based on percentages and concepts. Concepts are reasons why we do things on offense. Whom are we trying to influence and attack and Why!

EXAMPLE OF BAD PLAY SELECTION

A few years ago I am watching a major college game on TV. On the very first possession of the game, Team A had the football in the scoring zone with 1st and 10 on Team B's 11 yard line. Team A could make a first down inside the 1 yard line.

Team A has a tailback who is a Heisman Trophy candidate. A great running back. One of the best in the nation. On first down, from the I formation, Team A gave the ball to the Heisman Trophy candidate off-tackle for a 7 yard gain. GREAT! On 2nd and 3 on the 4 yard line, Team A ran a busted play or what may have been a down the line option, but the QB ends up gaining 2 yards anyway. It is now 3rd and 1 on the 2 yard line going in.

Remember, the game is in the first 2 minutes. Team A still have the Heisman Trophy candidate in the backfield. What does Team A do? Team A on 3rd and 1 on the 2 yard line going in…..lines up in the Shot Gun and throws a pass into the end zone.

Guess what? A receiver is wide open, BUT, he drops the pass! WOW! Now it is 4th and 1 on the 2 yard line. Team A still only needs 1 yard for a first down inside the one.The Heisman Trophy candidate is still at tailback but Team A decides to go for the field goal (just because a team goes for a field goal up close, doesn't mean the field goal is automatic).

If Lee Corco was watching, he must have had a heart attack. The field goal is blocked and Team B now gets the ball on their own 30 yard line. Here was a great example of poor play selection. Team A STOPPED THEMSELVES. COACHING BREAKDOWN!

But the story isn't over. Team B proceeds to fumble the ball on their first down play and Team A recovers the fumble. What luck. Team A gets the ball back for another opportunity in the 4 down zone.

Now….*Team A does not fool around.* On first down, with the ball on Team B's 30 yard line, Team A gives the the ball to the Heisman candidate who runs down to the 4 yard line. First and Goal on the 4. Team A again gives the ball to the Heisman candidate who takes it in for a TD. No fooling around here.

Why didn't Team A do this on their first possession? Who knows? You decide!

Here is another great example of *BAD PLAY SELECTION.*

Again I am watching two Division 1 teams play on TV. Team A has the ball on offense. They have the ball in the 4 down zone on Team B's 40 yard line. It is 1ˢᵗ and 10. Team A breaks the huddle. The QB NEVER....I repeat NEVER reads the defense to his right side. On his right is Team A's split end. The split end is being covered by a defensive back in what appears to be a bump and run defensive alignment. The defender is right on the receiver's nose.....right on the line of scrimmage. The QB NEVER sees this. On the snap, the QB stands tall and drills a pass to his right to the split end who steps back on what appears to be a wide receiver screen. The split end catches the ball 2 yards deep in the backfield but is immediately tackled by the defender covering him for a 2 yard loss. The defensive back almost intercepted the pass.

On 2ⁿᵈ and 12, Team A runs off-tackle for a 7 yard gain to create a 3ʳᵈ and 5 situation.

Now here was an example of poor play selection on first and second down and an error by the QB for not reading the defense on first down to see that the screen pass play had no chance for success. The defensive back almost intercepted the pass. The QB should have called an audible on first down.... and maybe the offense should have used the running play that gained 7 yards....on first down!

So here we see several BREAKDOWNS of this POSSESSION.

QB didn't pre-snap read the defense. Coach could have called the 2ⁿᵈ down off-tackle play on first down....why not? No audible was called by the QB ......if they the offense even had an audible system in place.

"More games are lost than won!"

I can give you hundreds of examples if space permitted.

18. GOAL LINE PACKAGE

The Goal Line Package......plays needed for the Red Zone...must be plays in all 3 categories (Direct, Delayed and Special).

The defensive team has their back up against the wall and usually has a tendency to fly to the football immediately due to the closeness of the ball to the goal line.

- First choice is to go DIRECT and see if they can stop you.

Remember the most vulnerable hole.....the off-tackle hole.

- If they stop you going direct, then be ready to;

    a. Play action pass off a direct fake.....or

    b. Use MISDIRECTION and try to get the defense continue flying to the ball. Take advantage of the misdirection of the defense.

Coach Woody Hayes, Ohio State legend......stressed...at the goal line.. "fake inside and go outside". Woody would come up in the *old fashion* T-formation and run the Belly Series or Drive Series. He had a great back in Pete Johnson (later with the Cincinnati Bengals) and he would fake Johnson inside and give to the second back or vice versa. Coach Hayes used this T-formation, when no one in America used the T-formation. He was not interested in being in VOGUE. *He was only interested in what he knew would work.* The concept is *sound.* The defense has to respect the first back due to the fact that the ball is so close to the goal line.

Thus, one of the BEST offensive concepts at the Goal Line is the use of the Triple Option. Many teams will never use the option due to the fact they have fear of hurting their QB. FEAR, did I hear someone say FEAR! Yes, FEAR controls many coaches and their play selection.

The following story is one in which I usually try to forget since we didn't score.

Back in the 1970's while at Plainfield High in New Jersey, we were playing the Westfield Blue Devils in our usual BIG Thanksgiving Game in front of 14,000 plus fans. Late in the fourth period with the score 3-0 in Westfield's favor. We march down to their half yard line. On fourth down, do we kick a field goal (no overtime period) or do we go for the score? "Bear" Bryant said a tie game was like kissing your sister. Since I did not want to kiss my sister, we went for the TD. I called a timeout before we ran our fourth down play. I told my team we were going to run a outside veer to the right. I told my QB that " their defense will tackle our diveback with three guys. Give a good mesh...a good ride....pull the ball and you will walk in the end zone or pitch the ball and the pitchback will walk in."

We ran the play and everything happened just as I predicted. The QB pulled the ball from the diveback and had an easy route to the end zone. What happens? Our QB slips and falls to the ground. His body falls over the goal line but I can see that the officials are NOT putting their hands up to signal a TD. Our fans are going wild. They think we scored. The officials said that our QB's knee hit the ground before he fell over the goal line. No score.

Westfield went onto to give us a safety. The game ended with us losing 3-2 in a football classic in front of over 14,000 fans.

BUT, the concept was good……..fake inside and go outside. They had the world tackle our diveback just as was expected. But, the mud played a trick on us and our QB fell.

Woody Hayes was always being criticized for using an offense that was "3 yards and a cloud of dust". But….THEY WON…..AND WON……AND WON!!!!!! Ohio State would run the football….and run the football…..

when they passed the ball (usually 3-4-5-6 times a game)….. they got great results. One or two TD passes a game and that is a fact. Not bad for a running team.

A GREAT RUN GAME requires great run blocking. Great run blocking requires much time in practice spent on run blocking. Run Blocking is PHYSICAL. Run blocking is HARD work. Run blocking creates TOUGHNESS. TOUGHNESS makes for tougher, better players. Coaches universally believe this, *BUT do they practice this concept in order to make it happen?????*

Some players complain they get hurt in practice. Thus some coaches tend to back off from such HARD WORK. A coach can back off from this HARD WORK....but he will never have the type of RUN GAME that is necessary.

To be a CHAMPION. You have to PAY THE PRICE.

19. 2 MINUTE OFFENSE

The 2 Minute offense..is a whole different Game Plan in itself. *The lack of REPS* in practice in this most important part of your game plan will most assuredly cause your team to BREAKDOWN.

The IMPORTANT concept for the coach to consider in the 2 Minute Philosophy is.......When do I go to it????? Why not when there is 5 minutes left rather than 2 minutes? The score of the game SHOULD dictate when to go to this strategy and NOT THE TIME left in the game or the half.

PROPER use of the clock is a very important concern. A BREAKDOWN here can kill you. Did anyone see the Super Bowl XL end of the first half or the end of the game? The Seattle Seahawks have a lot of explaining about their TIME MISMANAGEMENT during that game. Even ole John Madden was perplexed to how the Seahawks mishandled the clock.

Breakdowns! More Games Are Lost Than Won!

2 MINUTE OFFENSE CONSIDERATIONS

The following list includes considerations for the *2 Minute Offense*

- Consider what will be the maximum number of plays that you can run in a minimum number of seconds based on the plays you practiced.

- Plan to use plays that will get you to opponents 20-25 yard line with 30 seconds still on the clock. (Especially if you need a field goal)

- Consider when you will work the MIDDLE of the field as compared to outside patterns to stop the clock.

- Decide on your selection of OUT patterns that will be used to stop the clock.

- Decide on what runs and screens you will use and when you will use them.

- Decide on how you will communicate your play selection to the team.

- Decide when you will HUDDLE and when you will SPIKE the ball.

- Decide when you will call MORE THAN ONE PLAY AT A TIME!

- Decide on how you are going to handle the possible HOT RECEIVER situation.

These considerations and decisions MUST be made and practiced to eliminate the possibility of a BREAKDOWN during this critical time of the game. Remember, ...*"More games are lost than won!"*

DEFENSE

I mentioned earlier in this book that I surveyed that more BREAKDOWNS happen on offense. Thus very little is mentioned about defense. But, I will dedicate this one chapter to Defense.

My observation is that most BREAKDOWNS on defense have to do with skills or the lack of. Some BREAKDOWNS are because of philosophy.

The following points mentioned are key points that we try to accomplish and they are what we try to evaluate when we evaluate defensive POSSESSIONS. Some of the points have already been mentioned in this book but they are worth mentioning again.

NEVER ON DEFENSE

Bear Bryant said- " we are never on defense....we are always on offense...."

Key Points-

1. On every down.....strip the football...the ball belongs to you.

2. This is a MIND SET! We must practice STRIPPING DRILLS if we expect to strip the football. No excuses!

3. More ways to score on defense than offense. Your Goal for every game......SCORE ON DEFENSE. We MUST give great RECOGNITION for outstanding defensive plays.

4. We want to *Give the QB what he doesn't want to see......* PRESSURE When I say PRESSURE, I do not mean that I expect to get pressure from my regular defensive front. When I say PRESSURE, I mean adding stunts by linebackers and defensive backs. Stunts should from everywhere....right, left and middle...inside and outside. PRESSURE means having one more defender rushing than the offense has blockers. This dictates TIGHT MAN COVER.

5. We MUST Cover the QB Escape Lanes...ALWAYS! NO EXCUSES. Defensive linemen must be taught how to SPY and PICK UP the QB and or backs releasing from the backfield. This technique adds to the success of your stunting game.

6. We MUST use Pre-snap reads…….*anticipation* is better than reaction. We MUST consider Down and Distance …..………eyes………weight distribution (body language). Defensive line must determine before the snap what pass rush technique they will use.

7. On Pass Rush- Linemen are to *never DANCE with blocker*….hands and feet are always moving. Line must learn to anticipate when to get hands high.

8. On Defense- Use the sideline…SAMMY SIDELINE has never missed a tackle. If the offense is going to run…. force them to the boundary…short side…..give them 18 yards, not the wide side where there is 36 yards.

9. Force the QB to pass the football to the SIDELINE. NEVER to the inside. Force the QB to make the longer pass….use Sammy Sideline.

   Certain defenses have safeties inside and encourage passes to be thrown inside assuming the safeties and inside line-backers will take care of business. This type of defense tries to get collisions and deflections.

   I believe this philosophy to be TERRIBLE. I never want a receiver to have an easy catch assuming that my defenders will make collisions and jar the ball loose, etc. I have seen hundreds of games where easy slant passes were completed and the defensive safeties blew the tackle and the receiver went for a score or big yardage.

   I WANT NOTHING GOING INSIDE. I WANT NO PASSES COMPLETED GOING TO THE INSIDE.

WE FORCE EVERYTHING TO THE OUTSIDE. FORCE THE LONGER PASS.

When I see a defensive corner align with his outside foot up, Looking or turned to the inside, I want to "throw up." This alignment allows for the receiver to get inside easily. It is frustrating for the defensive front to exert great effort only to have easy passes caught over the middle.

By forcing longer passes, you force the QB to hold onto the ball longer and give your defensive front a better chance to get to the QB. Besides QB sacks, QB HITS are very important. Beat up the QB. Don't make it easy for him.

10. Force the QB to scramble-

The percentage of completed passes goes down dramatically when the QB has to throw the football ON THE RUN. QBs are taught that it is best to settle their feet down before throwing.

FORCE THE QB TO THROW ON THE RUN!

11. Prevent defense

We all have heard the funny, "Prevent defense prevents you from winning." Man...is this true! I have seen so many games in 47 years where a Prevent Defense has allowed the other team an opportunity to go down the field successfully and win the game.

I use two types of "so called prevent defenses".

1. In our 33 or 35 defense ...we play tight man cover on all 5 eligible receivers and keep our free safety 20 yards

deep so he can break on the ball and cover sideline to sideline. This defense has been very good to me in the 47 years I have been coaching.

2. In our Cover 5 we use 2 deep free safeties, 5 men in man cover and a 4 man rush. If our opponent goes to an empty backfield, on occasion we will FIRE a free safety to add a 6ᵗʰ man to the rush vs. their 5 blockers. This has been very successful for us.

This book is not about X's and O's....it is about concepts..... but I do feel that I need to mention the two coverages outlined above.

The BIGGEST BREAKDOWN that I have observed over the years is......IMPROPER DEFENSIVE ALIGNMENT.

One of the *first* things that I learned about defense was that if you want to play great defense.....you have to be in proper defensive alignment.

Thus in evaluation of defensive possessions, the first area I always evaluate is.......where we in proper alignment before the snap of the ball?

Then I evaluate execution and FINISH. Did the player FINISH the play or did he turn around and watch the end of the play and become a FAN?

"More Games are Lost Than Won".....is the truest statement that was ever made about why teams win or lose.

RECOGNITION

THE IMPORTANCE OF RECOGNITION IN WINNING!

Recognition is most important in creating and maintaining high team morale. A player always likes to know that he is doing well and that his accomplishments and contributions to the team are being recognized. Thus, *Recognition* helps to build self-esteem and in turn better self-confidence.

Every coach knows the importance of the MIND and how it affects his players. A higher level of self-confidence helps the player to have the ability to RECOVER quickly during a game when negative plays occur.

This concept helps us to OVERCOME BREAKDOWNS QUICKER.

Remember what Lombardi said, " we do not coach football…..we coach people."

We use Recognition in the following areas;

- Goal setting..both individual and team

When Goals are met we *Recognize* this achievement and establish new goals.

- Grading

Offense and Defensive Grades are given after every game.

- Achievement-

We use a helmet decal system. Since 1961 I have used one inch Red Stars for 21 different game time achievements. Everything from recovered fumble to Key Tackle, Key Block etc. A list is posted on the locker-room bulletin board and everyone can see who is doing what and who the team leaders are in the different categories. The players love this system.

Some negative minded coaches have said to me that they are concerned that the player is more interested in his Red Stars than if the team won the ball game. I do not believe this. We teach are players a "mind set" that we give recognition for INDIVIDUAL ACHIEVEMENT WITH OUR GOAL BEING.... INDIVIDUAL ACHIEVEMENT LEADS TO TEAM ACHIEVEMENT.

When coaching on the professional level, I could not use helmet decals. We still used charts on the bulletin boards and the players responded in the same positive fashion.

PLAYERS WANT RECOGNITION.

HIGHLIGHT THE UNSUNG HEROES

A football team always has UNSUNG HEROS. The QB, the running backs, the receivers.....all get plenty of recognition through the news media. The linemen and others receive very little recognition. Thus, when you as a coach use RECOGNITION as a positive Mind Set developing technique, you are stressing the importance of ALL PLAYERS and NOT just a select few that the media choose to highlight and recognize.

The linemen, especially on offense, usually are the UNSUNG HEROS that get the least recognition. In the NFL, every team has a great QB....great receivers....great running backs.....etc., but the teams that have the best offensive line are the teams that usually end up in the Super Bowl.

The fans know the names of the QBs...the running backs... etc., ...the names that get in the newspapers. But.....do the fans know the names of the offensive linemen?

Once I got smarter as a coach, I started to stress to my teams that the most important unit on the offensive side of the ball was the offensive line. Without a great O line...the QB can not pass......the running backs can not gain yardage.

When O.J. Simpson broke the 2000 yard rushing barrier in the NFL, he had the good sense of going on TV with the offensive line and stating "these are the guys that made it happen."

We SELL the importance of our offensive line by using this important concept of RECOGNITION.

OUR #1 GOAL

Our #1 Goal is to have FUN. Getting RECOGNITION is FUN. Thus FUN helps our positive mind set. Our positive mind set helps us to RECOVER from adversity….from BREAKDOWNS quicker and thus we have a better chance to WIN!….

"Hey Coach…..How do you Win?"

Hopefully…you had FUN reading this book. I had FUN writing this book. Hopefully there is a lot of MEAT in this book that you can use in your future coaching.

Good Luck to you!

Coach Theo

Milt Theodosatos

My second book, "Positive Mind Set…..Special Mind Set" is dedicated to a personal development program that I had to develop through the years to overcome the negativity that existed when I took over losing programs.

God Bless You and your efforts!

Coach Theo

Milt Theodosatos

Printed in the United States
144453LV00002B/68/P